The Uses of the Media
by the Chicano Movement

Francisco J. Lewels, Jr.

The Praeger Special Studies program—utilizing the most modern and efficient book production techniques and a selective worldwide distribution network—makes available to the academic, government, and business communities significant, timely research in U.S. and international economic, social, and political development.

The Uses of the Media
by the Chicano Movement
A Study in Minority Access

Praeger Publishers   New York   Washington   London

PRAEGER SPECIAL STUDIES IN U.S. ECONOMIC, SOCIAL, AND POLITICAL ISSUES

Library of Congress Cataloging in Publication Data

Lewels, Francisco J
   The uses of the media by the Chicano movement.

   (Praeger special studies in U. S. economic, social,
and political issues)
   Bibliography
   1. Mass media and Mexican Americans.   2.   Mass
media—United States.   3.   Mexican Americans—Politics
and suffrage.   I.   Title.
P92. U5L4   301. 16'1   73-22052

PRAEGER PUBLISHERS
111 Fourth Avenue, New York, N.Y. 10003, U.S.A.
5, Cromwell Place, London SW7, 2JL, England

Published in the United States of America in 1974
by Praeger Publishers, Inc.

To my parents
whose unfailing love and faith has made
all things possible

This is a very personal story about a people who have struggled for acceptance and security in a land that, to them, is often cold and hostile. It is the story of my own grandparents, who were forced to escape by horse-drawn wagon to a strange and distant land, in order to live in peace, away from the violence that ravaged the country they loved. It is the story of how nearly 8 million Mexican-Americans have lived in, fought for, and died in a country that has kept them in virtual isolation from the mainstream of its culture. It is also a story about the most complex society in history and how its social system can be used to the betterment of all its people.

One vital element in this society, integral in the socialization process for all Americans, is its system of mass communication. Even now, Americans are barely becoming aware of the enormous influence that the media have on their mores, their prejudices, their tastes, and their culture. Thus, it is not surprising to find that the Mexican-American minority (whose problems stem from an inability to communicate) failed to see the media's potential, until only a few years ago. The awareness grew as the black civil rights movement brought to the surface problems that had been dormant, or had simply not been communicated, for many years. Although the blacks led the way, the fight was always that of the brown as well, for, just as the blacks, Mexican-Americans have been the objects of systematic discrimination.

As a journalist, then, it was most logical for me to choose to write the story of how the media have served my fellow Mexican-Americans. Who better to do so than one who has lived in, and loved, both cultures, and who is, in fact, a blend of both? To say that this effort was possible without the assistance of many people, however, would be totally misleading. I therefore take this opportunity to express my deep-felt gratitude through a formal acknowledgment: to Dr. Ralph L. Lowenstein, professor of journalism, and my adviser at the University of Missouri, for the inspiration to set high goals; to Dr. Paul L. Fisher, director of the Freedom of Information Center, for helping me formulate my thoughts; to Nick Reyes, for pointing me in the right direction; to Gilbert Pompa, for giving me the opportunity to spend a summer of research with the U.S. Department of Justice; and to Bill Selden, who cared enough about my project to spend many hours of his valuable time, sharing his delightful and extraordinary insights.

Special acknowledgments are due the many people in the countless community-groups who took me into their confidence and allowed me to see the picture from the inside. Without their aid, the project would have surely been doomed. An estimated 250 letters, reports, interoffice memos, and other documents from the files of the Community Relations Service of the U.S. Department of Justice were read and many of them incorporated in this study. This was done through the cooperation and assistance of Gilbert Pompa, director of the National Services Division, and Willis Selden, chief of the Communications Section, of the Community Relations Service. I would also like to express my thanks to Joe Quintana and Martin Callery, two extremely bright journalism students at the University of Texas at El Paso, who assisted me in some painstaking research. And finally, I will always be grateful to Margaret Bell Sido, who stood by my side through the entire ordeal and gave me much-needed encouragement and support.

For all errors of fact and opinion, I bear the sole burden.

CONTENTS

LIST OF ABBREVIATIONS

ASH	Action on Smoking and Health
BBCMM	Bilingual Bicultural Coalition for Mass Media
BEST	Black Efforts for Soul in Television
CCOSS	Cabinet Committee on Opportunity for the Spanish Speaking
CTIC	Cable Television Information Center
CPA	Chicano Press Association
CAGS	Citizen Action Groups
CCC	Citizens Communications Center
CEETRUTH	Coalition for the Enforcement of Equality in Television and Radio Utilization of Time and Hours
CCOMMSS	Colorado Committee on Mass Media and the Spanish Surnamed
CSO	Community Service Organization
CROM	Confederacion Regional Obrera Mexicana
CARISSMA	Council to Advance and Restore the Image of the Spanish Speaking
CFFI	Dallas-Fort Worth Coalition for the Free Flow of Information
CRS	Community Relations Service
EEOC	Equal Employment Opportunity Commission
FCC	Federal Communications Commission
FDA	Food and Drug Administration
HELP	Home Education Livelihood Program

IRA	Interstate Research Associates
IMAGE	Involvement of Mexican-Americans in Gainful Endeavors
LAUD	Latin Americans in United Direction
LULAC	League of United Latin-American Citizens
MAPA	Mexican-American Political Association
MALDEF	Mexican-American Legal Defense and Education Fund
MANO	Mexican-American Nationalist Organization
MASO	Mexican-American Student Organization
NAB	National Association of Broadcasters
NAEB	National Association of Educational Broadcasters
NCMC	National Chicano Media Council
NCCB	National Citizens Committee for Broadcasting
NFWA	National Farm Workers Association
NMAADC	National Mexican-American Anti-Defamation Committee
NUC	National Urban Coalition
OEO	Office of Economic Opportunity
PASSO	Political Association of Spanish-Speaking Organizations
SIN	Spanish International Network
UCC	United Church of Christ
UMAS	United Mexican-American Students

The Uses of the Media
by the Chicano Movement

THE MEXICAN-AMERICAN
COMMUNITY: A CROSS SECTION

THE COMMUNITY IDENTIFIED

In mid-April 1972 a bizarre hijacking took place that most Americans found difficult to understand. In fact, most people who heard about this unusual plane hijacking could see little difference between Ricardo Chavez Ortiz and any other hijacker, regardless of his motives.

But Ortiz was no ordinary hijacker. Small, unimposing and dark-complexioned, he boarded the airliner that day for one purpose—to gain access to the nation's mass media in order to draw attention to the plight of the Mexican-Americans. His plan was to gain control of the aircraft and to return it with its passengers unharmed after he was allowed to talk to members of the press. In his mind, this was the only way that he could adequately express his freedoms of speech and press, guaranteed him by the First Amendment to the Constitution. Yet, even this did not work. His efforts resulted in little publicity that shed light on the problems of the second largest minority, and the entire point of his exploit was missed by the mass audience he sought to influence—one that was more concerned with the increasing number of hijackings than with the problems of any minority.

In part, this book is an attempt to answer the one question that was never asked by the media or by the public during this unfortunate incident. What caused a person to resort to such desperate means to express his views in a country that prides itself on having the most sophisticated communication system in the world and that boasts complete freedom of speech and press?

The answer is not a simple one; the roots of the problem lie buried in nearly two centuries of misunderstanding, conflict, and racism between a predominantly Anglo-Saxon majority and an Indian-Spanish minority, which, for a multitude of reasons that did not obtain

1

with other Caucasian minorities, has found it nearly impossible to assimilate into American society. The problem also lies, in part, with a communication system that caters to the majority, is owned and operated overwhelmingly by Anglo-Saxons, and is plagued by the basic dilemma of trying to serve all Americans while being forced (for economic reasons) to satisfy the tastes of the mass audience.

But before the issue of the media can be discussed, the problem must be put into perspective. Just who are the Mexican-Americans? Why and how are they different? What do they want? These are some of the questions that must be answered before any understanding can be reached with regard to the American mass communication system and its ability to serve this particular segment of the population. Hopefully, the reader will begin to know Ricardo Chavez Ortiz and understand the desperation that characterized his illegal efforts—the same desperation that gave birth to the Mexican-American civil rights movement.

MEXICAN-AMERICANS: GEOGRAPHY AND NUMBERS

The story could easily begin in Uvalde, Texas, 85 miles west of San Antonio in the hills of Edwards Plateau, where half the population of slightly over 10,000 is Mexican-American. The elegant homes and shaded streets that the tourist sees from U.S. 90 tell only half the story. The other half is the barrio (slum), clusters of shacks assembled piece by piece from salvaged junk, unpaved streets that are impassable when it rains and raise clouds of dust when it doesn't. This is where Uvalde's other half lives, mostly without sanitation, running water, electricity, or heat. At one corner of the city is the "barrio of the thirsty ones," given the name because the municipality does not supply water to the area since it lies just outside the city limits. Mrs. Juanita Gonzales, her husband Daniel, and their five children live there in a tar-paper and sheet-metal shack with a dirt floor.

Three times a week Mrs. Gonzales loads a 10-gallon can onto an old wheelbarrow and trundles it down to the Uvalde city cemetery where she fills it quickly from a garden hose. Once, she encountered an Anglo woman visiting a grave who told her not to get water from the cemetery any more; now she makes sure no one is around when she performs her household chore.[1]

According to U.S. Census Bureau figures, Mrs. Gonzales is one of nearly 6.2 million Mexican-Americans and one of nearly 7.8 million Spanish-speaking people in the United States today.[2] The latter figure represents approximately 4 percent of the nation's total population, with the great majority of them living in conditions similar to, or slightly better than, those of the Gonzales family. However, the above figures have been protested by Spanish-speaking organizations, particularly those active in the Chicano Movement, on the grounds that they do not represent a true picture of the Spanish-speaking American. The protesters say that there are as many as 7.5 million Mexican-Americans and nearly 15 million Spanish-speaking people in the U.S. today. Indeed, the task of counting Spanish-speaking people is not an easy one. Many women have married men with non-Spanish surnames; some men have changed their names to sound more Anglo; others came from Mexico with European last names, but still consider themselves Mexican-Americans; and millions of others have entered the U.S. illegally. All of this makes working with statistics on Spanish-surnamed individuals hazardous, yet no other data are available.

Most Mexican-Americans live in five of the nation's Southwestern states. The population figures and percentage of total population within each of these states indicates the potential political power that they have in the Southwest: Arizona (333,348) 19 percent, California (3,101,589) 16 percent, Texas (2,059,671) 18 percent, New Mexico (407,286) 40 percent, and Colorado (286,467) 13 percent. (Appendix A lists population by state.) And, even though they make up only 3 percent and 1 percent of the total populations of Illinois and Michigan respectively, the total Mexican-American population in those states (364,397 and 120,687) is nearly half a million.3 The fact is that Mexican-Americans have migrated to every state in the Union, clustering in industrial centers such as Chicago, Detroit, and New York. Today, 80 percent of the Mexican-American population lives in urban areas. Many immigrants became farm workers, hard-rock miners, or laborers on railroad construction gangs, forming settlements along the fruit and vegetable belts, around mines, and near railroad tracks. A good example of the drawing power of jobs away from the Mexican border is Chicago, with its farming country and railroad lines. The city and its surrounding area houses more Spanish-speaking Americans than any other city outside the Southwest—300,000 in the city and 150,000 in the surrounding area.4

The migration of Mexican-Americans to Chicago began in the early 1900s and grew slowly until the 1940s when thousands began settling there to fill jobs created by the war. Like Mrs. Gonzales in Uvalde, most of them found a meager existence awaiting them in their new world. Most of Chicago's Mexican-American population lives in the squalor of a slum area called Pilsen, a traditional port of entry for ethnic groups, which they inherited from others before them—the Jews, the Irish, the Germans, and the Bohemians.5

But despite their foreign appearance and language, a substantial number of Mexican-Americans can claim historical precedence over the Anglo. Santa Fe, New Mexico, was founded eleven years before

3

the Pilgrims landed on Plymouth Rock, and Spanish missions were established along the Pacific Coast while English settlers were fighting Indians on the Atlantic. Many Mexican-Americans can trace their ancestry to the Spanish explorers; their families lived in the Southwest for generations before the territory became part of the U.S., after the Mexican-American War. In fact, it is estimated that 1,333,000 Mexican-Americans are descendants of settlers who lived in the West and Southwest as far back as 1848.[6] Hundreds of thousands of others emigrated to the U.S. in the wake of the 1911 Mexican Revolution and never went back. To this day there is a steady flow of Mexicans into this country, both legally and illegally. The United States Immigration and Naturalization Service recorded 568,470 legal immigrants from Mexico between 1960 and 1972 and 6,463,547 legal nonimmigrant entrants between 1963 and 1972.[7] Unofficial sources estimate that from 2 million to 10 million entered the country illegally between 1910 and 1965.[8] Illegal entries continue to plague the U.S. Border Patrol, which finds it impossible to patrol the hundreds of miles of border where, for instance, a person can cross the often-dry bed of the Rio Grande within the city limits of El Paso, not only undetected, but without getting one's feet wet.

In the fiscal year ending June 30, 1972, a total of 64,040 Mexican aliens were admitted to the U.S. legally. Of these, 26,243 went to live in cities with a population of over 100,000 and 37,661 went to cities with populations of from 2,500 to 99,999. Los Angeles is the city named most often as the alien's permanent, established residency.[9]

Actually, Mexican-Americans can be categorized into three main groups. First, there are the descendants of settlers who arrived in the Southwest before the Mayflower reached the New World. These people live for the most part in rural communities scattered across New Mexico and Colorado.[10] The second, larger group is made up of those whose descendants migrated to the U.S. during the Mexican Revolution and up to about 1930. It is estimated that 1 million Mexicans settled in this country from 1910 to 1930.[11] Most of these either settled in border cities such as El Paso and San Diego or traveled farther to cities like Denver, Los Angeles, and San Antonio. The third group is the migrant farm worker who enters specifically to work, earn a substantial (for him) amount of money, and then return to Mexico. But despite their hopes of returning, many migrants end up staying. As a matter of fact, most Mexicans who settle in the U.S. think of their move as an expedient; unlike immigrants from Europe, they believe they can always go back home if things don't work out. Because of this psychological hold that Mexico has on them, sociologists say, many Mexican immigrants never really cut their ties with their motherland and only halfheartedly commit themselves to American culture. This ambivalence, along with white rejection of this quite different minority, sociologists argue, combined to place the Mexican-Americans, along with blacks, on the lowest rungs of the socioeconomic ladder.

A SEPARATE CULTURE

Mexican-Americans brought with them and maintained over the decades their own separate culture, language, values, and system of social stratification. In 1850, at the end of the Mexican-American war, the Treaty of Guadalupe Hidalgo acknowledged the annexation of Texas by the United States and ceded to the United States the territory that is now California, part of Arizona, and part of New Mexico. Mexican nationals were given one year to decide whether they wanted to move to Mexico, or remain in their homes and become U.S. citizens. The treaty guaranteed the property rights of these nationals as well as freedom of religion and choice of language. The approximately 75,000 Mexicans who decided to remain and receive American citizenship had a system of social stratification that, under Spanish rule, had controlled Mexico for more than 300 years.[12]

At the top were the peninsulares, those who were born in Spain and who had come to the New World as government, religious, or military leaders. Next were the criollos, Mexican-born people of Spanish parents (mostly fair-skinned, with little or no Indian blood). These became known as la gente bien (the people who are well off), la gente de razon (the people who reason), la gente decente (the decent people), and los que mandan (the people who command).

Below the criollos were the mestizos, those of mixed Indian and Spanish blood, now popularly known as la raza (the race). This class has always been in the majority in the Mexican-American community and has been able to achieve a limited amount of social success according to their appearance and coloring. It was, and still is, easier for el blanco (the white one) to be successful than for el moreno (the dark one). Comprising the lowest class was the Indian. Together with the impoverished or uneducated mestizos, the Indians were laborers, soldiers, artisans, and cowboys.[13]

The significance of the foregoing discussion is twofold. First, Mexican-Americans are not as homogeneous a group as might be generally believed, and second, the racial pressures exerted on this culture still exist to a great degree today. Furthermore, the color boundaries have been reinforced during the 150 years since the signing of the treaty by the need to compete in a predominantly white society. Unlike the black minority, many Mexican-Americans, due to the lightness of their skin, have been able to assimilate into white society and become accepted socially, in most cases at the price of forsaking

5

their own culture. However, for the bulk of the Mexican-Americans
(for reasons to be discussed later) assimilation into American society
has been a difficult, degrading, and traumatic experience.

The major difference, or at least the most obvious one besides
skin color, between Mexican-Americans and other Americans, is
language. Regardless of skin color or ability to sever psychological
ties with Mexico, nearly all Mexican-Americans, to some extent, have
had to cross the language barrier in order to succeed in an Anglo
culture. In this regard, sociological studies have found that Spanish
continues to be used to a high degree by most Mexican-Americans,
even by the younger heads of households and their children.[14] It has
been found that an overwhelming majority of Mexican-Americans
consider Spanish as their first language and English to be of secondary
importance; Spanish is learned first and English later; and Spanish
is spoken more fluently than English. In Texas, 40 percent of the
Mexican-Americans are considered functionally illiterate (in English),
while in Los Angeles only an estimated 25 percent can speak English
fluently.[15] The reasons for this phenomenon are several, according
to sociologists. It is partly blamed on the high degree of homogeneity
in socioeconomic status that prevails among the bulk of Mexican-
Americans. (As mentioned before, there is heterogeneity in the group
as a whole, but those who are light-complexioned and who can speak
flawless English are in a minority.) Other reasons for the century-
old language problem are the steady influx of immigrants from Mexico,
the freedom of movement between Mexico and the U.S., the strong
Mexican-American subculture, the spatial isolation of Mexican-
Americans, and the Mexican-American concept of la raza.[16] But by
and large the biggest blame today is being placed on the American
educational system, which for so long tried to force-feed English and
Anglo culture to youngsters who spoke only Spanish in the home. In
many places in the Southwest even today, Mexican-American children
are punished for speaking Spanish in school, and it wasn't until 1969
that students at an almost totally Mexican-American high school in
El Paso were able to get a rule abolished that forbade the speaking
of Spanish on the school grounds.[17] Researchers have found that this
attitude on the part of those who run the Anglo-dominated school
systems in the Southwest has the effect of causing students to feel
inferior, because of their language, and it discourages students who
are forced to compete with Anglos in what amounts to a foreign
language (English).[18]

It is only recently that educators in the Southwest have begun
approaching the problem as a cultural one and have attempted to teach
English as a second language, from the pre-first-grade level. The
problems of education and cultural assimilation will be discussed
further in the next two sections.

SOCIOECONOMIC CHARACTERISTICS

Many studies have been made in an effort to describe the Mexican-American culture and the socioeconomic status of its members. One of the problem areas inevitably focused on is the educational system as the primary socializing institution.

Indeed, education is described by the President's Cabinet Committee on Opportunity for the Spanish Speaking (CCOSS) as the most pressing deficiency in the Spanish-speaking community.[19] From the 1960 census and other private studies, the committee compiled some interesting statistics. In the Southwest, Spanish-speaking persons 14 years of age and older average 3.9 years less schooling than the Anglo and 1.6 years less than the nonwhite population. Counts of Spanish-speaking males 14 years old and over were found to have high percentages of persons with no schooling at all. These ranged from 5.3 percent in Colorado to 16.0 percent in Texas. Also, in Texas, 64.7 percent of Spanish-speaking Americans do not complete grade school. In Arizona it is 52.1 percent and in California it is 37.4 percent.

Few Spanish-speaking Americans go to college. Although they constitute 15 percent of all persons under 25, they represent only 6.2 percent of the total college enrollment. The percentage of Spanish-speaking males with a college degree ranges from 1.8 percent in Arizona to 2.8 percent in California.[20]

A sampling of statistics from other sources also indicates the poor education of most Mexican-Americans. It has been found that adults over 35 years of age average 7.3 years of schooling compared with 12 years for the general population, while one out of every five Mexican-American adults never attended school at all.[21] Although college enrollments are rising, total Mexican-American enrollment remains disproportionately small. For example, San Diego State College, which had 40 Mexican-American students in 1966, had 800 in 1971—out of 27,000 total students. This college is located in an area heavily populated by Mexican-Americans. It is also interesting to note that of 22,000 graduates in 1968 from the top five Southwestern universities, only 600 were Mexican-Americans.[22]

Most recently, the United States Commission on Civil Rights conducted "The Mexican-American Education Study" in order to evaluate "the nature and extent of [equal educational opportunities] for Mexican-Americans in the public schools of the Southwest."[23]

The first findings of this study, released in April 1971, support the previous studies. It concluded that Mexican-American school children are "severely isolated by school district and by schools within individual districts." Mexican-Americans are largely underrepresented on school and district professional staffs and on boards of

7

education, while most Mexican-American staff and school board members are found in predominantly Mexican-American school districts.

It was found that of the 2 million-plus Spanish-surnamed students in the U.S., 1.4 million or 70 percent are enrolled in the five Southwestern states mentioned before as having the bulk of the Mexican-American population. In these states, Mexican-American students comprise 17 percent of the total public school enrollment. However, only 4 percent of the teachers, 3 percent of the principals and 7 percent of the professionals employed in school district offices are Mexican-American.

In regard to their performance in public schools, the report summarized its findings about Mexican-American students:

> Without exception, minority students achieve at a lower rate than Anglos: their school holding power is lower; their reading achievement is poorer; their repetition of grades is more frequent; their overageness is more prevalent; and they participate in extracurricular activities to a lesser degree than their Anglo counterparts.[24]

Another major area for concern is employment and income levels for Mexican-Americans. The median income for Mexican-American families was $7,100 a year as compared to $10,200 per year for "white" families (Mexican-Americans included).[25] Nationally, 1.4 million Mexican-Americans are earning wages below the poverty guidelines set up by the Office of Economic Opportunity (OEO). Poverty-level guidelines call for a maximum annual income of $1,950 for a single person and $6,470 for a family of seven or more. A family of four is classified as poor if it has an income of $3,968 or less per year.

In 1970, the Census Bureau reported that Mexican-Americans accounted for 10.1 percent of the labor force that was unemployed, compared to 6 percent for the nation. Also, nationally, the 997,000 working Mexican-Americans were employed as follows: 18.2 percent white collar, 62.5 percent blue collar, 11.1 percent service workers, and 8.3 percent farm workers.[26]

Perhaps even more critical is the level of employment in government jobs. Statistics in this area were thought to be so out of proportion by Congressman Edward R. Roybal (D-Cal.) that he joined the League of United Latin-American Citizens (LULAC) and the American GI Forum in suing the federal government for job discrimination, on October 22, 1971.[27] Roybal claims that there is a virtual caste system in the federal government that excludes the Spanish speaking. He found that although comprising 6 percent of the total U.S. population, the Spanish speaking make up 2.9 percent of total federal employment and only one-third of one percent of its executives. The government would have to provide 80,000 jobs for the Spanish speaking to achieve parity.

In California, the Spanish speaking comprise 16 percent of the state's population but only hold 5.6 percent of local federal jobs (mostly at lower levels). The higher the Civil Service grade level, the fewer Spanish-speaking employees are found. During 1970, only .7 percent of all federal positions GS-13 through 15 were held by Spanish-speaking peoples and only .3 percent of the jobs over GS-15.[28] In the Washington, D.C., area, only .4 percent of the total federal work force is Spanish-speaking and of this figure some 40 percent are secretarial or clerical workers. Those agencies whose programs are likely to affect the great majority of Spanish-speaking people have some of the government's lowest percentages of those very people. The departments of Housing and Urban Development (HUD), Health, Education, and Welfare (HEW), Labor, Commerce, Transportation, Veterans Administration, Interior and Agriculture average 1.4 percent Spanish-surnamed.

Economic problems such as these cause other problems. The Spanish-speaking American is seven times more likely to live in substandard housing than his Anglo counterpart. The mortality rate at birth or during the first years is twice that of the Anglo and the average life span of the Spanish-speaking American, in Colorado for example, is 56.7 years as opposed to 67.5 years for everyone else. The average life expectancy of a Spanish-speaking child born to a migrant family is 38 years. Among the migrants, 41 percent of the deaths occur by the age of 5.[29]

Because of the low employment figures of Mexican-Americans in law enforcement and because until recently this minority had practically no power base in the Southwest, a perpetual problem has existed between the Spanish speaking and the police and judicial system. In the Southwest, about 7.4 percent of the total uniformed personnel in 232 agencies are Spanish-speaking. In Phoenix, 95 percent of all trials have no Spanish-speaking Americans sitting on juries. In Los Angeles County, where there are nearly 500,000 eligible Spanish-speaking residents, only four served as grand jurors during a period of 12 years.[30]

ASSIMILATION AND THE MELTING POT MYTH

When Dr. Jack Forbes, sociologist, testified at the U.S. Commission on Civil Rights hearing in San Antonio, Texas in 1968, he was asked by the General Counsel, "Why hasn't the Mexican-American assimilated in the Southwest?" He answered, "Excuse me, sir, but that is the wrong question. Why hasn't the Anglo assimilated?"[31] Perhaps the point Forbes was trying to make was that not only are Mexican-Americans equal in numbers in some places in the Southwest to the Anglos, but they were there first and, whereas most can speak some English, relatively few Anglos can speak Spanish. The attitude that the counsel was verbalizing is basically the same that former U.S. Commissioner of Education, Harold Howe II, believes is dominant in the white, Anglo culture:

> [Our society] equates Anglo-American origin and Anglo-American ways with virtue, with goodness, even with political purity. Other cultures are not merely different; they are inferior. They must be wiped out, not only for the good of the country, but for the good of the child. Not only must he learn to speak English; he must stop speaking anything else.[32]

But despite this Anglo attitude, if Howe's theory is to be believed, Mexican-Americans have not assimilated into the Anglo society for the most part; a distinctive Spanish-Indian-Mexican culture survives in the United States. The melting pot idea that assumes the assimilation, integration, and amalgamation of diverse racial and ethnic groups has just not worked, particularly with Americans of African or Oriental racial backgrounds as well as with Mexican-Americans.

Social scientists have attempted to study and describe the system of social solidarity among Mexican-Americans and some conclusions have been reached. Some point out that acculturation is hindered by their desire and ability to hold on to their Mexican cultural heritage because they feel that it is too precious and universally valid to be abandoned.[33] Others analyze the problem in terms of kinship systems, familial ties, community, spatial isolation, and homogeneity in socio-economic status. But, according to some, all of these are interrelated with what they consider to be the most important dimension of social solidarity. This is the concept of la raza, or "the race," which is a special kind of unity that joins all Latins in a cultural and spiritual bond derived from God. (The use of the Spanish language is the primary symbol among Mexican-Americans of loyalty to la raza.)[34]

Those of Indian ancestry (estimated to be more than 90 percent of Latin-Americans) have always identified closely with this concept, but since the growth of the Brown Power or Chicano Movement, the term has tended to divide the Mexican-American people. Those who had managed to achieve a high degree of assimilation into Anglo society suddenly found the youthful Brown Power Movement telling them to be proud of their Indian ancestry, something they had had to abandon in their effort to gain Anglo acceptance.

According to Dr. Daniel Valdez, who prefers to be called Hispano-Americano, those white people (like Mexican-Americans) who are farthest removed from the northern European cultural mold are given only a qualified Americanship. He believes that as one gets farther from the English-Scottish Protestant core of the original Anglo-Saxon culture in America, the more likely one is to be thought of as foreign.[35] Thus, many Mexican-Americans have gone to great lengths to appear less "Mexican." Philip Montez, writing in the Civil Rights Digest, relates the story of a college friend who fell in love with a blonde Anglo girl in California during the 1950s. Before consenting to the marriage, the girl's father required that the young man change his name from Martinez to McKeever, which he did. When he was married his parents were not allowed to attend the ceremony because they didn't speak English and they would have ruined the desired illusion.[36] Today, the youth movement argues that no person should have to sacrifice his own personality and cultural identity in order to become assimilated.

Closely related to the concept of la raza is the controversy surrounding the choice of terms to describe Mexican-Americans. Throughout this book the term Mexican-American is used consistently because it is a factual term that applies to all Americans of Mexican descent. However, it is by no means the preferred term of many Mexican-Americans, despite its factualness. Many people today prefer the term Chicano, which most experts agree was derived from the way the Indians used to say Mexicano, changing the "x" to a "ch." The term implies an Indian heritage, thus its popularity among the Brown Power advocates and its distastefulness to those who have been trying to forget their Indian ancestry. Probably, the majority prefers to be called just plain American. But since Anglos have found it necessary to use hyphenated names for people who don't look Anglo, most would prefer to be referred to as Mexican-American (although in New Mexico Hispano is sometimes preferred).

The term Spanish-American is resented because of its obvious intention in the Southwest as a euphemism for the word "Mexican" which Anglos mistakenly feel will offend.[37]

For the purpose of this study, the term Mexican-American will be used unless reference is made to members of the Chicano Movement who obviously prefer the term Chicano.

MEXICAN-AMERICANS ORGANIZE

The problem of dealing with the customs and laws of the United States caused Mexican-Americans to form an almost uncountable number of organizations. The oldest of these are the mutual benefit societies; they have existed at least as long as the Treaty of Guadalupe Hidalgo. These societies attempt to protect members from the necessity of dealing with the larger community by providing death benefits and sometimes insurance against accident or sickness. Even today, their clubhouses and halls are often still the center of the Mexican-American communities.[38]

Some members of mutual benefit societies began to gain influence as businessmen in the growing Mexican-American communities in the 1920s. These businessmen also began to turn away from the idea of death benefits toward that of civic service. The best example of this kind of middle-class organization is the League of United Latin-American Citizens (LULAC).[39] In 1928, LULAC was formed in Harlingen, Texas, to provide a central organization for several local mutual benefit societies, and has since evolved into a civic service organization dedicated to assimilation. The LULACs now have chapters throughout the U.S. with their center of strength lying in Texas. The goals of the LULACs reflect their public image of conservatism; they are openly patriotic to the United States and actively seek to adopt its culture. They also retain some of the ideas of the self-protection groups by proclaiming their opposition to discrimination.[40] Young militant groups feel that the LULACs and other "establishment" organizations have failed to improve significantly the plight of Mexican-Americans.

In 1928 the Confederacion Regional Obrera Mexicana (CROM), a Mexican industrial union associated with the American Federation of Labor, encouraged two unions in California: one was centered in Los Angeles and the other in Brawley in the Imperial Valley. La Union Trabajadores del Valle Imperial was organized to give Mexican farm workers a bargaining agent. The union tried to fight the contract system under which most crops were planted, tended, and harvested in the Imperial Valley.[41]

The Los Angeles union encouraged by the CROM was the Confederacion de Uniones Obreras Mexicanas. Like the Imperial Valley union, it was organized in 1928. The union had about twenty locals in Los Angeles, San Bernardino, Ventura, Riverside, and Orange counties. Its demands were similar to those of the Imperial Valley strikers, especially against labor contractors.

An organization through which Mexican-Americans sought to participate in American democracy is the Community Service Organization (CSO). It grew out of a committee formed in 1947 to elect Edward Roybal to the Los Angeles City Council. Although it failed in this first attempt, it was undoubtedly the deciding factor in Roybal's subsequent election in 1949.

However, the CSO is not primarily interested in electing Mexican-Americans to public office. Its basic aim is to provide political

12

representation for those who would be otherwise unrepresented and, toward this goal, it has organized and participated in many projects, such as voter registration.

Some of the new projects concern consumer education. They began as a simple neighborhood organizing effort and have developed into a buyers' club, consumer complaint center, and credit union. The center employs several full-time organizers and VISTA volunteers who also work with a work-experience program and a youth-leadership project. In addition, the CSO now publishes a small newspaper to keep members informed of its activities.[42]

Another organization that operates in a manner similar to that of the CSO is the American GI Forum of the United States. It is a Mexican-American veterans' group first organized in Corpus Christi, Texas, in 1948. At that time Mexican-Americans were refused service in public places and generally forced to attend segregated schools. Attempts of Mexican-American veterans to join veterans' organizations were either refused or met with the suggestion that they form their own, separate chapters. Mexican-American veterans, who served in the United States armed forces as equals, especially resented this discrimination, but it was one specific insult that led to the formation of a Mexican-American veterans' organization.

When the family of a dead Mexican-American war hero applied for a plot in a local cemetery, the request was refused. Officials informed the family that the cemetery was for white people only. Mexican-American veterans were insulted, and some of them brought the incident to the attention of the President of the United States. Although arrangements were made for burial of the soldier in Arlington National Cemetery, the insulted veterans decided to insure against a recurrence of such an event by organizing to end discrimination against Mexican-Americans. Under the leadership of Dr. Hector Garcia, they began the Forums.[43]

The first Mexican-American group openly to proclaim itself political was the Mexican-American Political Association (MAPA). It was organized in 1959 to be the active, "hell-raising" arm of the Mexican community. The purposes set for it were to seek "the social, economic, cultural and civic betterment of Mexican-Americans and all other Spanish-speaking Americans through political action."[44]

Other similar organizations followed. One is called The Political Association of Spanish-Speaking Organizations (PASSO). Its outstanding success was achieved in Crystal City, Texas, in 1963. Crystal City was a town of about 10,000 people; about 7,500 of them were Mexican-Americans, although they exercised little voice in city government. In the 1963 election, PASSO, supported by the Teamsters Union, organized Mexican-Americans to pay their poll tax and vote for a slate of Mexican-American candidates. The slate was headed by Juan Cornejo, the Teamsters' business agent, and it won the election.[45]

13

Student organizations have also been created. Perhaps the best-known of these groups are the United Mexican-American Students (UMAS) and the Mexican-American Student Organization (MASO). UMAS is a confederation of clubs in which each has individual autonomy to determine its degree of militancy. They have been active in pressing for Mexican-American studies programs in individual high schools and colleges. UMAS has also sought more opportunities for Mexican-Americans in higher education.[46]

Militancy in the rural Mexican-American community began formally on September 17, 1965, when the National Farm Workers Association called a strike against grape growers in Delano, California.[47] Urban Mexican-Americans took their first militant action on March 28, 1966, with the Albuquerque Walkout. That was the time and place set for a meeting between national Mexican-American leaders and the federal Equal Employment Opportunities Commission. When the leaders arrived, they found only one commissioner present and none of their previous complaints had ever been acknowledged; so they walked out. A press release explaining this action sounded a new tone. "The nation's five million Mexican-Americans will begin marching and demonstrating on a national scale unless the government takes immediate steps to provide them with equal educational and employment opportunities."

Urban Mexican-Americans began implementing this statement by their support of the National Farm Workers Organizing Committee. It was set up by Cesar Chavez who approached it from a background of organizing for the Community Service Organization. He combined CSO ideas with traditional labor union tactics.[48]

In 1967 the federal government created the Inter-Agency Committee on Mexican-American Affairs, a special agency that would concern itself with the issues and needs of Mexican-Americans.[49] Its purposes were to assure that federal programs would reach the Mexican-Americans, to provide the assistance needed to seek new programs to handle their exceptional problems, to serve as an ombudsman within the government for the Mexican-Americans, and to be the central liaison point between the communities and the federal officials.

Because the Inter-Agency Committee needed a sense of continuity in order to perform its advisory and advocative roles effectively, legislation was introduced to make it a statutory agency. Included in the bill was a new agency name: "The Cabinet Committee on Opportunities for Spanish-Speaking People." The new agency title reflected the expanded scope of the committee. The committee's legislative mandate directed it to encompass the affairs of all Spanish-speaking Americans: Mexican-Americans, Puerto Ricans, Cubans, and others. On December 18, 1969, Congress passed the bill establishing the new committee and, on December 30, President Nixon signed the bill into law.

The major areas of concern for CCOSSP are: the advocacy
of equal employment opportunities for the Spanish speaking in the
federal government; equitable distribution of federal services; programs
and funds to meet the needs of the Spanish speaking; and the providing
of technical assistance in program areas designed to meet the unique
needs of the Spanish speaking.[50]

THE FARM WORKERS' MOVEMENT

Only three real leaders have emerged who have been able to
evoke widespread support and action among Mexican-Americans in
the lower socioeconomic strata. The first and foremost of these is
Cesar Estrada Chavez, 45, organizer of the farm workers union and
spiritual leader of la causa (the cause) (otherwise known as the Mexican-
American civil-rights movement). The other two are Reies Lopez
Tijerina, organizer of New Mexico's Alianza Federal de Pueblos Libres
(the Alliance of Free Cities) and Rodolfo (Corky) Gonzales, creator
of Colorado's Crusade for Justice.

But Chavez is undisputably the most important figure, because
of the immense popularity he achieved as the leader of the farm
workers and because the unionization of the migrants has a much
deeper significance to Mexican-Americans than an ordinary strike.
The much deeper meaning of la huelga (the strike) was revealed in
the amount of national coverage it received both during the grape strike
and, later, during the lettuce boycotts. A writer for Time magazine
in 1969[51] remarked that the grape strike had none of the qualities
normally required to get such national attention—it must threaten the
supply of essential goods and services, it must have a great impact
on the economy, or it must have spectacular bloodshed. The grape
strike had none of these, yet it and the accompanying boycott, according to the writer, "clearly engaged a large part of the nation."

Indeed, Chavez's union numbers only 25,000 at the height of the
harvest season and it directly affects only a small portion of the nation's Mexican-American population (and that portion is isolated in
rural areas, while most Mexican-Americans live in urban areas).[52]
Perhaps the secret of the popularity of the strike and the national
movement that it started lies in the personality and values of Cesar
Chavez, without whom the unionization of the farm workers might
never have succeeded. The problems he faced in organizing migrant
workers seemed insurmountable in 1952 when he became associated
with the Community Service Organization. Chavez saw his most serious
obstacle before him as the century-old effort of California farmers
to depress wages and undercut resistance by pitting one group of
poor people against another.[53]

By the 1860s, the Indians who were used as near slaves in Spanish California had all but disappeared and had been replaced by Chinese labor. Chinese immigrations was ended by the Chinese Exclusion Act of 1882, and after that, the farmers turned to the importation of the Japanese. The Japanese were then bitterly resented, because they undercut all other labor. The next wave of farm laborers in California were the Hindus, the Arabs, the Armenians and the Europeans. After 1910, starving Mexican refugees presented the growers with a new source of cheap labor, which, because it was there illegally, had the additional advantage of being entirely defenseless. During the 1920s, Filipino labor was brought in to undercut the Mexican laborers. Most of the Mexican nationals were deported after 1929, when the Arkies and Okies produced a labor surplus in the California fruit fields.[54] By 1942, the Chinese had moved to the cities, the Japanese had been shut up in concentration camps, the Europeans had graduated from the labor force and become farmers, the Anglos had filled jobs in factories, and those workers left were not enough to harvest crops. This emergency was met by a series of agreements with the Mexican government known as the bracero (field worker) program, under which large numbers of Mexicans were brought into California from Mexico for harvesting. After the war, Washington lobbyists for the growers convinced the government to continue the program, arguing that Americans would not do the hard stoop labor required. In a way, the argument was valid; not many would work for the 60 cents an hour that the desperate Mexicans were willing to accept, thereby undercutting indigenous workers. By 1959, about 400,000 foreign workers were working in the U.S. despite the fact that 4 million people here were unemployed.[55]

What few people today realize is that the effort to organize the farm workers was in a way a battle between U.S. citizens (Mexican-Americans) and noncitizens (Mexican nationals). Even though almost half of the members of Chavez's union were not citizens, it was the Mexican national who became the strikebreaker and who posed a real threat to the success of unionization.

A MOVEMENT GROWS

This, along with the itinerant lives of the farm workers, made Chavez's chances of success seem slim. But nevertheless, he took his $1,200 in savings and started the National Farm Workers Association (NFWA) in 1962 with headquarters in the San Joaquin Valley agricultural town of Delano. He soon created a death benefits plan for his members, a credit union with $35 in assets (by 1969 it had more than $50,000), and a union newspaper called El Malcriado (the bad boy),

16

which quickly rose to a circulation of 18,000.[56] At stake, he felt, was a battle in behalf of the entire Mexican-American population, for if the farm workers could succeed, then those in the cities could also. This belief was the main reason for lack of agreement between Chavez and the growers. They saw themselves as management in a classic labor dispute, while Chavez and his followers believed that la causa was at stake—the plight of all Mexican-Americans.

In order to achieve the goal of unionization, Chavez was willing to dedicate his entire life to the cause. Throughout the movement he, his wife, and their eight children lived in a small two-bedroom house in Delano, subsisting on $10 a week from the union and on food from the communal kitchen in the nearby union headquarters.[57] His willingness to live a stoic existence, his strict adherence to nonviolence, and his deep religious beliefs, many believe, were the main elements in transforming the unionization efforts into a national movement. His determined leadership was often put to the test.

Once, with police watching, Anglos marched up and down the picket lines slamming the strikers with their elbows, kicking them, stomping their cowboy boots down on strikers' toes, cursing them, spitting on them, and brushing them narrowly with speeding trucks. On September 23, 1965, a striker was knocked down repeatedly by a grower before the police intervened. Chavez had warned them that he could not control the crowds if the harassment did not stop. According to a report of the incident in the Fresno Bee, the police dispersed the crowd "when one picket fell down." They also arrested strikers, who were taken into custody for such offenses as shouting, using a bull horn in public, using the word "huelga" and, in one case, for reading publicly Jack London's "Definition of a Strikebreaker."[58]

By the same token, Chavez was not always able to prevent his followers from striking back. Reports of packing sheds being set on fire, foremen being threatened, and tires being slashed were not uncommon.[59] But, for the most part, Chavez was able to avoid bloodshed by placing emphasis on nonviolent means of publicizing the cause.

UNIONIZATION AND THE MEDIA

Although publicity was always an important factor in the movement, the need for nationwide publicity became imperative when Chavez decided to resort to the boycott to keep pressure on the table-grape growers. He applied it first in 1967 to the Giumarra Vineyards Corp., the largest U.S. table-grape producer. Giumarra began using the labels of other growers, in violation of the Food and Drug Administration rules, to circumvent the boycott, and, in retaliation, the strikers had to appeal to stores and consumers throughout this country, Britain, and Scandinavia not to buy California grapes.[60] The task was monumental for the poorly financed strikers, particularly in view of the fact that the growers had commissioned the J. Walter Thompson advertising agency to place $400,000 worth of ads extolling the benefits of table grapes, and the California public relations firm of Whitaker and Baxter to advise the growers about how to counter the boycott. Whitaker and Baxter helped to manage Richard Nixon's unsuccessful campaign for governor of California in 1962 and handled the American Medical Association's efforts to defeat Medicare.[61]

Mark Day, author of Forty Acres, estimates that the growers spent between $7 million and $10 million on public relations and advertising throughout the movement. They tried to tell the public the growers' side of the strike by sponsoring all-expense paid tours of the Delano vineyards for community leaders throughout the nation and Canada. Their chief aim was to change the issue from "worker rights" to "consumer rights."[62]

One year after the boycotts began, nationwide grape sales were off 12 percent and a year later they were down as much as 15 percent. Shortly thereafter, 10 of the growers (about 12 percent) announced that they would negotiate a contract with Chavez.

Much of this success can be attributed to Chavez's uncanny instinct for making the public aware of the deeper meaning of the movement. In February 1968, Chavez, in the midst of the grape strike, began a 25-day fast as an act of penance and to recall workers to the nonviolent roots of the movement. During the fast, Chavez was called to court in Bakersfield on charges of improper picketing. While he was in the courtroom, 2,000 farm workers knelt outside in prayer, and in March, when he ended his fast, approximately 8,000 joined him at the Communion ceremony. Kneeling next to him in Delano's Memorial Park was Robert Kennedy. Both Kennedy and Reies Lopez Tijerina gave speeches, and Paul Schrade, on behalf of the United Auto Workers, presented the union with $50,000 for the construction of its new headquarters at a site called Forty Acres.[63]

The fast, although no doubt religiously inspired, had a tremendous effect on the movement and the nation. It had the immediate effect of drawing the strikers together, and it disputed the growers' claims that the union efforts had no following. Some people attended Mass every night of the fast at the Forty Acres where Chavez was staying, coming 65 to 80 miles a day. Others waited one or two hours to talk with him, and he took the opportunity to talk with as many as he could.[64] But even more important, the attendance of Senator Kennedy and the ensuing publicity brought the strike before the public in a way that could never have been achieved through violence or through carefully planned public relations.

18

According to Mark Day, the nightly Masses caught the attention of national TV audiences, which he feels won the movement considerable national support. And he describes the scene at the courthouse this way:

> Over a thousand farm workers and several clergymen sur-
> rounded the courthouse, singing the strike song, De
> Colores (of colors), and praying together. The judge and
> the entire staff at the courthouse were on edge. Jerry
> Cohen, the chief legal counsel for [the strikers], and I
> supported Cesar as we entered the building. He was ex-
> tremely weak and barely made his way throuth the crowd.
> Newsmen and TV cameramen were tripping over each
> other as we made our way up an escalator to the court-
> room. As we entered the courtroom, a very well-dressed
> and very hostile woman in her forties drew close to Cesar
> and spat out, "I hope you get what's coming to you, you
> son-of-a-bitch!" I later saw her leave the courthouse in
> a new Cadillac, which bore a bumper sticker that read,
> "America, Love It or Leave It!" The trial was post-
> poned by the nervous and angry judge. The charges were
> later dropped.[65]

Another well-publicized event was the workers' march from Delano to the steps of the capitol at Sacramento. The Pregrinacion (pilgrimage), as it was called, was inspired partly by the freedom march from Selma, Alabama, the year before, but like the fast that Chavez was to undertake two years later, it was also religiously symbolic.[66] Its emblem was the Mexican patron saint of the campesinos (peasants), La Virgen de Guadalupe (the Virgin of Guadelupe), which was to arrive with the workers on the capitol steps on Easter Sunday. Chavez organized it as a penitential march, as an atonement for past sins of violence on the part of the strikers.

The march was scheduled to begin on March 17, 1966, but John Dunne's account of the event tells how it very nearly did not make it out of Delano.[67] The chief of police in Delano had heard about the march in a Newsweek story and had prepared for the event. As the day approached, he was told that the procession would walk down Albany Street, which skirts the town, but on the day of the march, the workers changed their minds and decided to walk through the center of Delano, led by Chavez. Immediately, a line of police blocked their route of march. But so many reporters and television cameramen were on the scene that the police chief and the city manager decided to avoid an incident and let the marchers go through town. "They wanted us to arrest them," the chief related to Dunne. "But that was

19

one time we just lucked out. They were all down on their knees with their priests saying all their words and what not. It would have made them look good if we arrested them with all that press and TV there. No, I got to say we just lucked out."[68]

On Easter morning they were joined by thousands of supporters and political figures. Despite the fact that Governor Pat Brown spent the weekend with Frank Sinatra in Palm Springs, the event drew the attention of the nation, for on this occasion it was announced that one of the fruit growers had agreed to negotiate a contract. When it was signed in June 1966, it provided an hourly wage of a dollar seventy-five and a union hiring hall. It was the first real contract for farm workers in the history of American labor.[69]

Another more recent march took place in May 1969—from Coachella, California to the international border at Calexico. The purpose of the march was to appeal people in Mexico to join the movement by not breaking the strike. The nine-day march began on May 10 with an outdoor Mass, despite the fact that the temperatures were in the hundreds. Each marcher was given a copy of the rules: "Obey the orders of the captain. Drink water sparingly. Do not wander from the line without permission. Do not talk back to agitators. Keep cool, baby, keep cool. Be cheerful. We are on the road to victory."[70] It soon became apparent that the rules were necessary. Large trucks would pass by at high speeds, passing only a few feet from the marchers. But the marchers had also been reminded by Chavez that this would be a pilgrimage of penance for past violence. He frequently told them that a union is built on suffering and sacrifice. "There are no short cuts. Nothing worth-while is ever won without suffering. To be a man is to suffer for others. God help us to be men," he told his followers during his fast. He felt that the marches would discipline the strikers, help them understand the meaning of nonviolence, and form them into a community of purpose and concern.[71]

On the morning of the eighth day of the march, the Reverend Ralph Abernathy of the Southern Christian Leadership Conference (SCLC) joined the pilgrimage, marched the entire morning with them and pledged that SCLC would help the farm workers. During the last two days of the march, the number of marchers grew from 75 to 500, including farm workers, students, housewives, ministers, priests, and nuns. Just outside of Calexico, a bus load of television and movie entertainers arrived from Hollywood. Another group joined them minutes later, including Senators Walter Mondale (D-Minn.) and Ralph Yarborough (D-Tex.). The march ended with a rally in a Calexico park. Cesar Chavez and Edward Kennedy each addressed the crowd of marchers and newsmen. Three weeks later, the Los Angeles Times reported that a small group of table-grape growers had agreed to negotiate with the union.[72] Apparently, when the plight of the farm workers was brought to the attention of the American consumer, enough of them chose not to buy what Mark Day calls "Grapes of Wrath."[73]

Incidents that were reported in the media often demonstrated the strikers' instinct for the strategic importance of confrontation and the authorities' insensitivity to the power of the press. One such incident occurred when Chavez attempted to accompany ten workers, whom he had persuaded to leave their jobs, back onto the company property to get their belongings. They were afraid to go alone, but the company representatives refused to allow NFWA members to trespass. With Wayne Hartmire of the Migrant Ministry and Father Victor Salandini, a Catholic priest, Chavez decided to chance arrest by trespassing. All 13 men were quickly arrested for trespassing, but, for no apparent reason, the San Diego County sheriff's representatives decided to strip all of the men naked, except Father Salandini, and chain them together. This time, the movement benefited from the overkill instinct of the authorities. When the episode was reported by the press, Chavez's legal guilt was obscured by the humiliating stripping of the men.[74]

While some were marching, others were distributing leaflets in front of supermarkets. Many of the leaflets featured a picture of a typical worker's shack in the San Joaquin Valley. Seated on the bed in the dwelling was a small Mexican-American girl, her clothes in tatters and a bare light bulb hanging from the ceiling. The caption read, "Please help the farm workers. Do not buy California grapes." In the cities, they used every possible technique to win public support. In Chicago, they held a sit-in at the headquarters of the Jewel Tea Company. Housewives wrote postcards and placed phone calls to the A & P executive offices in Philadelphia. In Toronto, they held balloon-ins at several supermarkets. Helium-filled balloons with "Boycott Grapes" painted on them were released in the stores or handed out to children. One volunteer quipped, "Have you ever seen a clerk try to relieve a child of a balloon?"[75]

In the end, the publicity generated by the boycott undermined the company's determination. Clergymen denounced growers from the pulpit, letters of protest poured in from more than forty states and housewives stopped buying grapes. The growers also began feeling pressure from the unions with which they had contracts. The combination was finally too much to overcome.

THE LOCAL PRESS AND THE MOVEMENT

From its very first issue, El Malcriado enraged many growers and citizens of Delano with its picaresque attacks against what its editors saw as the injustices pervading the community. The paper, published in English and Spanish, combated the growers, who were supported by the established press of the area. It also attempted to educate the workers on the significance of the strike. Cartoons by Andy Zermeno portrayed the structure of the California agricultural and rural society graphically. The growers were represented by El Patroncito (the boss), a fat, vulgar-looking man in sunglasses, with a panama hat. Labor contractors were portrayed by Don Coyote, and the workers were pictured by Don Sotaco, a humble, downtrodden campesino. The cartoons propagandized the workers' cause and educated newcomers on the moral, economic, and political issues of the strike.[76] John Dunne, who studied the strike as an outsider, was amazed at the ignorance that prevailed in both camps about the other side. According to him, El Malcriado didn't help in breaking down the harmful stereotypes that the strikers had about the growers:

> Nowhere was this [ignorance] more apparent than in El Malcriado, the strikers' newspaper, which has as little regard for fact as a Citizens for Facts broadsheet. [A citizen's organization set up to investigate the strikers.] In the first issue I read, I saw an item about women being used as bribes, offered to male employees as a reward for a vote against the NFWA.[77]

But if there was misinformation, it was because the two camps had never communicated. Most workers had never been to the East Side, where the Anglos lived, and most Anglos had never even seen Cesar Chavez or been on the other side of the tracks.

The local papers did little to hide the fact that they supported the growers. The Coachella Valley Sun, edited by Gale Ellis, president of the Coachella Chamber of Commerce, often butted heads with the union leaders. His paper was accused of taking a propaganda position supporting the farmers when it printed a John Birch Society petition to deny the union the use of public facilities. Two union leaders in 1968 pleaded with the paper to print both sides of the story. Ellis called the leaders "threatening agitators" and the two retaliated by leading a group of pickets in front of the Sun offices that read: "Gale Ellis is Prejudiced," "The CV Sun is Sour Grapes" and "Don't Buy the C.V. Sun."[78]

But overall, the battle of the local media had little effect on the outcome of the strike and the movement. The issues were national in nature and the strikers, with uncanny accuracy, were able to take advantage of the press coverage they received. This fact was probably the foremost reason that the unionization efforts succeeded—and it was to be a prelude to a much more active role by the growing Chicano Movement in the mass media.

The miraculous success of the farm workers also had a profound effect on the Mexican-American population, particularly those who had already identified somewhat with the Chicano Movement. In 1969, Chavez commented on the inspiration that the union's efforts caused in the youth of California, "Five years ago . . . nobody wanted to be Chicanos. They wanted to be anything but Chicanos. But . . . I went up to San Jose State College and they had a beautiful play in which they let everybody know that they were Chicanos and that Chicano meant something and that they were proud of it."[79] Yet curiously, Chavez is against some of the main principles of Chicanismo. He believes that the traditional way of proving one's machismo (manliness) through violence is in error. "La causa must not risk a single life on either side, because it is a cause, not just a union, and has to deal with people not as membership cards or social security numbers but as human beings, one by one."[80] He also criticizes the ideological basis of la raza, "la raza is a very dangerous concept. I speak very strongly against it among the Chicanos. At this point in the struggle [1969] they respect me enough so that they don't emphasize la raza, but as soon as this is over they'll be against me, because I make fun of it, and I knock down machismo, too. . . . I don't like to see any man discriminating. But when a Mexican discriminates— ooh! That really cuts me. As a Mexican-American, I expect more of them than of anybody else. I love them, and I guess I'd like them to be perfect."[81]

THE BROWN POWER MOVEMENT:
A MATTER OF PRIDE

Brown Power is an ideology born as a vague idea inspired by the Black Power Movement, nurtured and encourage by the successes of the farm workers, and thrust violently on an unsuspecting America at a time when few people even realized that there was a second minority. It can be described as an awakened sense of pride among a people, who for so long have found little of which they could be openly proud. To some, Brown Power is a life condition, shared by all Mexican-Americans; it is a feeling that is created by being a Mexican in a sea of Anglos.[82] There is automatic membership for those who are of la raza and who are not ashamed of their Indian heritage and their brown skin. It is also an expression of pent-up anger and frustrations toward a society that has rendered Mexican-Americans powerless to improve their standard of living—poor education, poor jobs, and the misery of life in the barrio.

As in most social movements, the vanguard of this one is composed of the most radical elements, with overtones of militancy and racism and an admiration for the aggressiveness and the sophistication of the Black Power militants. But, even though this segment has threatened violence and at times delivered its promises, the Brown Power Movement has not demonstrated as much potential for violence as the Black Movement. Its most influential leaders bear little resemblance to Stokely Carmichael. Cesar Chavez, who relied heavily on student support during the farm worker movement, advocates nonviolence and detests racism of any kind. Reies Tijerina, like Chavez well over thirty, is also a supporter of peaceful social change, despite his knack for getting into trouble with the establishment. And by and large, the Mexican-American community as a whole has little sympathy for the violent aspect of the Negro protest as well as for those who aspire to involve Mexican-Americans in a replay of the Watts riots in which two Mexican-Americans were killed.[83]

Even many so-called militants would rather not resort to violence to achieve goals. One Chicano youth put it this way: "We found that colleges were paying attention to the blacks because they were militant, so we started to get as militant as the blacks." Another adds, "I hope we don't have to get as militant as the blacks. But if we have to, we will."[84]

In essence, the Brown Power Movement was the first stage in the long fight for civil rights. Today, the larger, more organized Chicano Movement encompasses a larger segment of older Mexican-Americans who, while adding moderacy to the movement, have gained, sometimes to their own surprise, a bit of militancy themselves. Through the enthusiasm and anger of the youth and the patience and wisdom of the older Chicanos, the movement has made enough social changes to reduce somewhat the need for much violence. But it was not always so.

Brown Power erupted for the most part in the schools of the Southwest in the form of protest walkouts, student marches, and picket lines all designed to bring to public attention the conditions of the schools in the barrios. From the high schools it moved into the colleges where Chicano students for the first time exerted themselves as a group. They began forming organizations that stressed pride in oneself and one's culture, and, like their black counterparts across the country, they began making demands on the schools for courses in Chicano studies, more Chicano faculty members and counselors, more scholarships and, most important, recognition on the part of school officials that a problem existed. Even as far back as the beginning of the grape strike, students at the high school in Delano, including the children of Cesar Chavez, organized protest marches. The trend spread throughout California and then to the rest of the Southwest. In 1968, in East Los Angeles, 13 Chicano students were arrested for organizing a boycott of their schools to protest what they thought were

24

intolerable conditions. In Livingston, California, 53 students skipped their high school classes on Mexican Independence Day (September 16) and demanded that it be made an official holiday. They also wanted the schools to hire Mexican teachers and counselors, and to offer courses in Mexican and black history. They wanted the double lunch periods ended in which white kids ate at the first sitting and black and brown at the second. It is interesting to note that in this period police picked up the truants, but when the big local farms need extra help at harvest time, the compulsory attendance law is ignored.[85]

At Fremont High School, in Oakland, students demonstrated for weeks to demand a Chicano student union and Mexican-American entertainment and speakers at assemblies. At Redwood High in Visalia, California, Chicano students made 21 demands on the principal, including Mexican food in the cafeteria, mandatory attendance by all teachers at classes in black and Mexican culture, and a rule to keep police, probation, and parole officers off the school grounds.[86]

Mexican-American students at Berkeley formed a student group called Quinto Sol (fifth sun) and marched in 1967 upon hearings of the U.S. Civil Rights Commission in San Francisco to protest the exclusion of Mexican-Americans from a program designed to recruit college students from minority groups. They also attacked the commission for having only one Mexican-American on its staff of 350, yelling "Practice what you preach! " until police threw them out. They also invaded and occupied the office of the university president at Berkeley to protest the purchase of California grapes by the university cafeteria; they were forcibly removed from the office and eleven were jailed. One of their more moderate projects is the publication of a quarterly review called El Grito (the cry) in an effort to communicate their ideas to other Chicanos as well as the establishment. In 1969 there were only 200 Mexican-American students out of a total enrollment of 25,000 at Berkeley.

By 1970, the student unrest stirred by the Brown Power Movement was approaching the critical point. And when school opened in East Los Angeles that year, a riot broke out in the community, which contains about 750,000 Mexican-Americans, after a march protesting the war in Indochina. Two men were killed, including Ruben Salazar, a columnist for the Los Angeles Times; to this day, Chicanos believe he was assassinated by police because of his sympathy for the movement.[87] A few days later, the National Mexican-American Anti-famation Committee in Washington, D.C., released the results of urvey that reported an increase in militancy and a "greater likeli- of violence" in nine cities with large Mexican-American popula- By January 1971, the tension in Los Angeles had once more ed a peak. More than 2,000 Chicanos, mostly students, massed nt of the city's police headquarters in a demonstration that erupted into a brick- and bottle-throwing melee. The riot continued through the main shopping area with rioters breaking store windows and looting. More than 30 persons were arrested during the skirmish.[88] The point was made quite clearly that the Brown Power Movement was indeed capable of violence and destruction, even though throughout the rest of the Southwest, young protestors managed to avoid violence.

One of the most publicized groups in this movement are the Brown Berets, formed in Los Angeles by David Sanchez during the farm workers' movement. Although they have affiliates throughout the Southwest, there is a separate group called the Texas Brown Berets of San Antonio. But even though they are thought of as one of the most militant of young Chicano organizations, much of their activity is centered around peaceful protests such as walkouts, picketing, and sensitivity programs for those who are ignorant of Chicano problems.[89] The Brown Berets are made to look rather tame by a group in San Antonio called the Mexican-American Nationalist Organization (MANO), a clandestine group that insists all "whites" are racist enemies who should be driven out of the Southwest, by force if necessary. Most of the members are ex-convicts or Vietnam veterans who have experience in demolition techniques and guerrilla warfare. Their leaders tell them to "Get guns wherever you can, preferably from addicts who steal them. Don't buy them, if you can help it, and don't carry them. Stay off dope. Don't use the telephone. Don't make public speeches. Get a job, if you can, and try to look harmless. This is how the Minutemen have survived. We will too."[90]

THE CHICANO MOVEMENT

Spurred on by the radical youth, the Chicano Movement has slowly drawn in the older, more moderate segment of the Mexican-American community—those who see a desperate need for rapid social change. Armando Rendon, in his book Chicano Manifesto, verbalizes the dreams that many of the current Chicano activists have. He says that rather than wanting to get into the American culture, the Chicanos want out:

Out of a cultural milieu which desensitizes man and woman into profit-producing machines, devoid of humanity and soul.

Out of a country which poses a military answer to every foreign issue, and despite having been born in revolution against Old World oppression, seeks to deny the same right to nations who reject Brave New World oppression.

Out of gringo patterns of injustice and prejudice which
have suppressed the best talents and minds of our people
and accepted only those few willing to gringoize themselves to achieve a measure of fulfillment.

Out of a system of government which is controlled
by economic and social influence to reap its benefits at
the expense of the poor and minority peoples.

To put this in positive terms, the Chicanos in
essence desire three things: to fulfill our peoplehood,
Chicano; to reclaim our land, Aztlan; to secure the future for ourselves and our countrymen.[91]

To achieve these, and other more specific goals, the movement
has made use of the courts, political organizations, demonstrations,
boycotts, and sometimes violence. And they use these tools to win
back their long-lost lands called Aztlan. Aztlan is actually the Southwest, where the ancient Aztec Indians lived before they migrated to
Mexico. To the Chicano, the southwestern part of the United States
is Aztlan, the spiritual home of the Chicano Movement.[92]

The concept of Aztlan is also associated with the effort to regain
land that was lost by those Mexicans who lived in the Southwest in the
late nineteenth century. Northern New Mexico, particularly Rio Arriba
County, has been the scene of bloody land wars since the first Mexican
settlers arrived in the seventeenth century. They killed and were
killed by the indigenous Indian population. Eventually, the Mexican
settlers were able to put down roots and to achieve and armed truce—
a coexistence with the Indians. Until the conquest of Mexico by the
United States, the people of the Mexican villages along the Rio Bravo,
the Rio Chama, and the Rio Grande were isolated. Their land had
been granted to them in common and in perpetuity by the Spanish and
Mexican governments. In the late nineteenth century, Americans
poured into Albuquerque, Santa Fe, and the river valleys and dispossessed, in large part, those whose ancestors had dispossessed the
Indians.[93]

Although the concept of Aztlan covers a much larger and vaguer
area, the current efforts of Reies Lopez Tijerina are the most serious
move to regain at least some of this lost land for the descendants of
the Mexican settlers of northern New Mexico. In order to accomplish
this goal, Tijerina formed an organization called the Alianza Federal
de Mercedes, now known as the Alianza Federal de Pueblos Liberes
(heretofore referred to as the Alianza). A former Pentacostal preacher,
Tijerina served a prison term for assaulting a forest ranger and
abetting the destruction of government property (part of an effort to
bring attention to the fact that the land once belonged to ancestors of
Mexican-Americans). At present, only 2 percent of the 100 million

acres covered by the 1848 Treaty of Guadalupe Hidalgo belongs to
direct heirs. The rest is divided between government and private
owners and includes, for example, the city of Albuquerque, New Mexico.

In another effort to make his point, Tijerina organized the in-
famous courthouse raid at Tierra Amarilla, New Mexico. It was an
effort to make a citizen's arrest of Alphonso Sanchez, district attorney
for Rio Arriba County, the man who was leading a legal-political
battle against the Alianza. Almost certainly destined to failure, the
act caused Tijerina to hide in the wild hill country of northern New
Mexico. Its most important effect was to recall the life that had
flourished in the Southwest before the Anglo came. That effort to
revive feelings for the lost peasant life struck the deep sense of pride
that many Mexican-Americans in the area feel. In some communities
in New Mexico, the Alianza has been successful in electing traditional
Mexican governments, headed by alcaldes (mayors). The significance
is symbolic, a parallel to the effort to revive a rural economy under
way in northern New Mexico. An organization called the Home Education Livelihood Program (HELP) was formed to establish an apple-
marketing cooperative, several woodworking cooperatives, and other
similar projects.[94]

The third major leader in the Chicano Movement, mentioned
earlier, is Rodolfo (Corky) Gonzales, a former prize fighter, bail
bondsman, and Democratic politician who formed the Crusade for
Justice in 1966. The Crusade's membership is young and is supported
enthusiastically by a large segment of the Chicano community, even
those who dislike the Spiritual Plan of Aztlan, which the Crusade sup-
ports. At the 1969 Chicano Liberation Conference, the Crusade for-
malized a plan denouncing "gringo" domination and calling for a re-
birth of the bronze people. The Crusade preaches autonomy and runs
a bilingual school, directs its own security force, operates several
small businesses, and is planning Chicano farms.[95]

In 1967, Gonzales drew attention to Chicano problems by running
for mayor of the city of Denver for the sole purpose of suing the victor
for violation of the election spending law. In this way, he was able to
subpoena 50 of Denver's leading citizens who "cooled their heels" in
courthouse waiting rooms until the judge ruled that the law was out-
of-date and moot. This was the beginning of La Raza Unida, at first
a loosely bound group of political organizations headed by Gonzales.
It began running candidates primarily to publicize Chicano grievances
but in southern Texas where Mexican-Americans constitute a majority
in many towns, they started winning.[96] Today, La Raza Unida is a
formal political party with broad support throughout the Southwest
from Mexican-Americans at both ends of the liberal-conservative
continuum.

LA RAZA UNIDA PARTY

From its very beginnings, the Mexican-American community
has tried to find ways of coping with the Anglo culture, and today, the
Chicano Movement has inspired a new approach. Corky Gonzales
expresses his ideas of building a Mexican-American power structure
based on nationalism:

> . . . let's take that common denominator, that . . . tool of
> nationalism, and utilize it to work against the system.
> Let's use it to work against the two parties that I say are
> like an animal with two heads eating out of the same
> trough, that sits on the same boards of directors of the
> banks and corporations, that shares in the same indus-
> tries that make dollars and profits off wars.
> We start it and call it an independent Chicano politi-
> cal organization. We can use it as . . . a forum to preach
> and teach. We can gain the same amount of radio and TV
> time as any phony candidate. We proved it in Colorado.
> I ran for mayor as an independent, and I campaigned two
> weeks. Two weeks, because we were busy directing a
> play and busy in civil rights actions. But we had the same
> amount of time on TV as anybody else, and on radio we
> were able to start to politicize people. We were able to
> start to tell about an idea.[97]

Within the Mexican-American community, Gonzales' call for
an independent party was considered a radical one. Traditionally,
the Spanish-speaking voters have voted (if they voted at all) in solid
Democratic blocs, but, until recently, there has been little fear by
politicians of either party that the Latin voters could join and have a
vital voice in American affairs. If they did, due to sheer numbers
alone, they could swing elections in a dozen or more major metropolitan areas such as New York, Miami, Denver, Los Angeles, and
Chicago. They could also be a powerful force in the states of Arizona,
California, New Mexico, Texas, Colorado, and New York, with a surprising total of 90 electoral votes.[98]
But despite the potential power, little of it has ever been realized.
In the Southwest there is not one large city with a Mexican-American
mayor, not one state with a Mexican-American governor, and only one
state with a Mexican-American senator (Joseph Montoya of New Mexico).
There are four Mexican-Americans in the House of Representatives.
In California there is one on the state legislature, but there is none
on the Los Angeles City Council, although more than 1 million Mexican-
Americans live in the area.[99] Gradually, though, politicians have

become aware of the growing political concern of the Mexican-Americans and the power that may realize its full potential in future years. In recent years, the Mexican-American vote has influenced elections in Texas, New Mexico, and California. Senator John Tower of Texas owed his election in 1966, it is claimed, to a general dumping of the Democratic candidate by Mexican-Americans as a protest to the Democratic party. In New Mexico, Governor Cargo has said that his first election was due to the anger of the Mexican-American voters at the Democratic machine, and, in California, the defeat of Hubert Humphrey in 1968 was paralleled by a switch in barrio precincts from a 95 percent Democratic vote to a 35 percent Republican vote.[100]

To activists in the Chicano Movement, the message was obvious: harness the power of the Mexican-American vote and use it as a bargaining tool with the two major political parties in areas where victory is impossible. This idea of a third political party crystalized in, of all places, Crystal City, Texas, a quiet farm town in South Texas with a population of around 10,000. Typically, it is divided by the railroad tracks; on one side live the farm workers who comprise 85 percent of the population and on the other live the Anglo ranchers who own 95 percent of the farms.[101]

It was here that Jose Angel Gutierrez, the son of a barrio doctor in the town, returned with a master's degree from St. Mary's University in San Antonio and officially formed La Raza Unida Party. While at the university, he founded the Mexican-American Youth Organization, which was funded by the Ford Foundation but later had the funds cut off because of political activities. Within a few months, the party startled Texas politicians by winning the school board election.[102]

Since that time, politicians have begun scrambling for the Mexican-American vote in the Southwest as they have never done before. Also, the party has found an unexpected enthusiasm from Mexican-Americans throughout the country. Gutierrez has made it clear that in Texas, where in many counties 85 percent are Mexican-Americans, La Raza Unida plans to take control of everything—judgeships, county commissioner posts, chamber of commerce seats, and even the Boy Scouts.[103] Throughout the Southwest Chicano youth organizations are helping the effort by running voter registration drives among the people of the barrios.[104]

However, not all Mexican-Americans are pleased with the drive for political, independent unity. Among the most critical opponents of movement is U.S. Representative Henry Gonzales (S-Tex.), who has attacked La Raza Unida as being a form of "reverse racism . . . as evil as the deadly hatred of the Nazis." He fears that intense loyalty to la raza could lead to riots in the barrios of Texas. He also stands for what many older Mexican-Americans believe and have worked for all their lives—assimilation. "I stand for classless, race-less politics." So far, no Raza Unida candidate has attempted to oppose him for reelection.[105]

So it is that the Mexican-American community today is caught up in a struggle between the youth, who are tired of waiting for change, and their elders, who have worked for and found a comfortable niche in the Anglo world and would rather not have anyone rocking their boat by focusing on old racial problems. But the generation gap may be narrowing. The activists today, particularly in the media, are in many cases older and better educated than they were a few years ago. The call for racial pride has struck the hearts of many Mexican-Americans who have for a long time been proud of their cultural identity, but were afraid to show it. This in itself may eventually cause a new wave of older, more moderate Mexican-Americans to join a movement that has already had a surprising number of successes.

NOTES

1. "Tio Taco Is Dead," Newsweek, June 29, 1970, p. 24.

2. U.S. Bureau of the Census, General Social and Economic Characteristics, Final Report, PC (1)-C1 United States Summary, June 1972, p. I-382.

3. Ibid., p. I-344.

4. "The Chicanos Campaign for a Better Deal," Business Week, May 29, 1971, p. 5.

5. "Americans in the Midwest," Chicago Magazine, Autumn 1969, p. 83.

6. Luis F. Hernandez, A Forgotten American (New York: Anti-Defamation League of B'nai B'rith, 1969), p. 8.

7. The United States Immigration and Naturalization Service, 1972 Annual Report, June 1972, pp. 51-53, 55.

8. "The Chicanos Campaign," p. 5.

9. 1972 Annual Report, pp. 46-50.

10. "Tio Taco," p. 23.

11. Hernandez, Forgotten American, p. 8.

12. Ibid., p. 9.

13. Ibid., p. 10.

14. R. L. Skrabanek, "Language Maintenance among Mexican-Americans," Civil Rights Digest, Spring 1971, pp. 18-23. Mary Mahoney, "Spanish and English Language Usage by Spanish-American Families in Two South Texas Counties" (unpublished Master of Science thesis, Texas A&M University, January 1967).

15. "The Little Strike That Grew to La Causa," Time, July 4, 1969, p. 34.

16. Skrabanek, "Language Maintenance," p. 23.

17. "The Little Strike," p. 34.

18. Roy Bongartz, "The Chicano Rebellion," The Nation, March 3, 1969, p. 271.

19. Carlos Conde, ed., A New Era, Cabinet Committee on Opportunities for Spanish-Speaking People (Washington, D.C.: U.S. Government Printing Office), Fall 1970, p. 3.

20. Ibid., p. 4.

21. "The Chicanos Campaign," p. 2.

22. U.S. Congress, Senate Committee on Equal Opportunity, Hearings on Equal Education Opportunity before the Select Committee on Equal Opportunity of the U.S. Senate, statement by Domingo Nick Reyes and Armando Rendon, 91st Cong., 1st sess., 1970 (Washington, D.C.: U.S. Government Printing Office, 1970), p. 928 AR.

23. Salvadore Carpio, "Commission Report on Mexican-American Education—What It Means," La Luz, May 1972, pp. 9-10.

24. Ibid., p. 10.

25. Social and Economic Characteristics, p. 75.

26. Ibid.

27. Edward R. Roybal, "Federal Caste System against the Spanish Speaking," Congressional Record, March 30, 1972, p. 142.

28. "Hispanos Grossly Under-Represented in Federal Jobs," La Luz, May 1972, p. 50.

29. Conde, A New Era, p. 5.

30. Ibid., pp. 6-7.

31. Philip Montez, "Will the Real Mexican-American Please Stand Up?" Civil Rights Digest, Winter 1970, p. 28.

32. Ibid.

33. Skrabanek, "Language Maintenance," p. 23.

34. Ibid.

35. Tom Pino, Ethnic Labels in Majority-Minority Relations (Denver: La Luz Publications, 1971), p. 57.

36. Montez, "Will the Real Mexican-American. . .," p. 29.

37. Pino, Majority-Minority Relations, p. 58.

38. Kaye Briegel, "The Development of Mexican-American Organizations," in The Mexican-Americans: An Awakening Minority, ed. by Manuel Servin (Beverly Hills: Glencoe Press, 1970), p. 161.

39. Ibid., p. 163.

40. Douglas Weeks, "The League of United Latin American Citizens: A Texas-Mexican Civic Organization," Southwestern Political and Social Science Quarterly, X (December 1929): 257.

41. Briegel, "Mexican-American Organizations," p. 165.

42. Ibid., p. 168.

43. Ibid., pp. 169-70.

44. Ibid., p. 174.

45. Ronnie Dugger, "Ballot-Box Revolution: The Political Awakening of Mexican-Americans in Texas," Frontier, September 1963, p. 7.

46. Briegel, "Mexican-American Organizations," p. 178.

47. Eugene Nelson, Huelga: The First Hundred Days of the Great Delano Grape Strike (Delano: Farm Worker Press, 1966), p. 65.

48. Briegel, "Mexican-American Organizations," p. 172.

49. Conde, A New Era, p. 9.

50. Ibid., p. 11.

51. "The Little Strike," p. 16.

52. "The Chicanos Campaign," p. 3.

53. Peter Matthiessen, "Profiles, Organizer P. I," The New Yorker, June 21, 1969, p. 45. (Note: Matthiessen's two-part series on Chavez is one of the best sources for in-depth understanding of the farm workers' movement.)

54. Ibid., p. 46.

55. Ibid., p. 47.

56. "The Little Strike," p. 17.

57. Ibid., p. 19.

58. Matthiessen, "Profiles, Organizer P. I," p. 72.

59. "The Little Strike," p. 19.

60. Ibid., p. 18.

61. Ibid., p. 19.

62. Mark Day, Forty Acres (New York: Praeger Publishers, 1971), p. 91.

63. Matthiessen, "Profiles, Organizer P.I," pp. 67-68.

64. Peter Matthiessen, "Profiles, Organizer P. II," The New Yorker, June 28, 1969, p. 63.

65. Day, Forty Acres, pp. 46-47.

66. Ibid., p. 45.

67. John Gregory Dunne, Delano (New York: Farrar, Straus and Giroux, 1967), pp. 131-32.

68. Ibid.

69. Matthiessen, "Profiles, Organizer P. II," p. 57.

70. Day, Forty Acres, p. 74.

71. Ibid., p. 75.

72. Los Angeles Times, June 14, 1969.

73. Day, Forty Acres, p. 77.

74. Dunne, Delano, pp. 146-47.

75. Day, Forty Acres, pp. 71-72.

76. Ibid., p. 44.

77. Dunne, Delano, p. 121.

78. Day, Forty Acres, p. 103.

79. Matthiessen, "Profiles, Organizer P.I," p. 70.

80. Ibid.

81. Matthiessen, "Profiles, Organizer P. II," p. 61.

82. Ralph Guzman, "The Gentle Revolutionaries," Selected Reading Materials on the Mexican and Spanish American (Denver: Commission on Community Relations, City and County of Denver, April 1971), p. 90.

83. Ibid., p. 91.

84. Bongartz, "The Chicano Rebellion," p. 272.

85. Ibid.

86. Ibid.

87. New York Times, September 17, 1970.

88. Washington Star, January 10, 1971.

89. El Paso Herald Post, December 27, 1971.

90. Wall Street Journal, November 6, 1970.

91. Armando Rendon, The Chicano Manifesto (New York: Macmillan Co., 1971), p. 10.

92. El Paso Herald Post, December 27, 1971.

93. Peter Nabokov, Tijerina and the Courthouse Raid (Albuquerque: University of New Mexico Press, 1969), pp. 1-25.

94. "Chicanos Campaign," p. 4.

95. Ibid.

96. Ibid.

97. Rodolfo (Corky) Gonzales, "Chicano Nationalism: The Key to Unity for La Raza," in A Documentary History of the Mexican-American, ed. by Wayne Moguin (New York: Praeger Publishers, 1971), pp. 379-80.

98. "U.S. Latins on the March," Newsweek, May 23, 1966, p. 35.

99. Stan Steiner, "Militance among the Mexican-Americans," The New Republic, June 20, 1970, p. 16.

100. Ibid.

101. Ibid., p. 17.

102. Ibid.

103. "Tio Taco Is Dead," p. 27.

104. El Paso Herald Post, January 10, 1972.

105. Steiner, "Militance among the Mexican-Americans," p. 18.

2

THE FIRST MEXICAN-AMERICAN PRESS

Traditionally, Mexican-Americans have had little regard for the Anglo press and vice versa. Wherever Mexican-Americans have clustered the media have done little to serve the Spanish-speaking populace, sometimes for valid reasons. Until recent times many Mexican-Americans have demonstrated little interest in participating in the Anglo social structure, and even if they have, they have been handicapped by the language barrier. As a result, those who have been able to speak and read English (those of the upper socioeconomic strata) have been forced to enter into a social and business world that has excluded their less fortunate compatriots, and the media have been content to let a sleeping Mexican lie. Even those who tried to reach the Mexican populace by publishing Spanish-language newspapers in the rugged pioneer days of the 1800s met with failure, in many cases because of an apathetic and illiterate audience.

It almost seems a contradiction, then, to find that the first printing press on the West Coast was established by a Mexican-American. When Agustin Zamorano set up the first press in California in 1834, the event marked the day that printing first spanned the United States.[1] Shortly thereafter, newspapers began publication in the settlements of San Francisco and Los Angeles and then in the smaller towns. That same year another Mexican-American set up the first printing press in New Mexico.[2] He was the Reverend Antonio Jose Martinez, a 24-year-old priest in Taos, New Mexico, who used his press as a forum for political and religious reform. He published a weekly newspaper called El Crepusculo (The Twilight) and printed books in Spanish on the alphabet, vocabulary, catechism, grammar, logic, and physics.

But, for the most part, Spanish-speaking people in the Southwest who were interested had to rely on the Anglo press for news of

American society, a situation that did not change much until the recent rash of Chicano Movement publications and a growing awareness in the more established Spanish newspapers. In the 1850s they could read La Estrella (The Star), which was the Spanish page of the Los Angeles Star, the first paper in that city. It began publication in 1851. Or they could read the Spanish page of the Southern Californian, started shortly after the Star in the same city. San Franciscans could read El Eco del Pacifico (The Echo of the Pacific), which was the Spanish page of a French weekly, or a Spanish-language newspaper called La Cronica (The Chronicle), which stopped publication in 1856.[3] But the newspaper that probably served Mexican-Americans best was El Clamor Publico (The Public Outcry), a Spanish weekly started by Francisco P. Ramirez in 1855.[4] Ramirez, a self-styled champion of Mexican-Americans in California, began as a printer's devil and compositor for La Estrella but established his own publication when he found that he could have no voice in the editorial policy of that paper. His new paper, Los Angeles' third paper, and its first in Spanish, was considered a milestone in the evolution of the Spanish-speaking people for it was the first to devote itself to their advancement. In expressing the Liberal-Democratic ethos of Jefferson and Jackson, he had to contend not only with all the disadvantages of printing a frontier newspaper, but with the hostility of the "gringos" and with the illiteracy of his audience.

Leonard Pitt, in his book The Decline of the Californios, describes the paper's other problems:

> As journalism, his paper left much to be desired. Editorials blended freely with news reports, until the reader could scarcely distinguish facts from analysis.

But on the other hand he praises the paper for its coverage:

> It nicely captured the distressed mood of the Latin-Americans in Southern California; it gave them remarkably good news coverage; and it gave them a public forum for their ideals.[5]

Another important chapter in the history of the Spanish-language press was written by Ricardo Flores Magon, who fled Mexico in the early 1900s, at the time of the Mexican Revolution, and settled in San Antonio, Texas. There he began a crusade against the tyranny of the Mexican dictator, Porfirio Diaz, with his newspaper La Regeneracion (The Regeneration).[6] For his comments against Diaz and his articles about Mexican-Americans, Magon was threatened with assassination and forced to flee to St. Louis and then to Canada. He finally settled in Los Angeles and began La Regeneracion once again. This time he was tried and convicted of sedition for an article he wrote calling for a labor movement of worldwide proportions. He was sent to the federal penitentiary at Leavenworth, where he died in 1922.

Despite the radicalism of these two examples, the Spanish language press has, for the most part, been exemplified by an orientation toward events in Mexico and Latin America rather than toward the problems of Mexican-Americans. Examples of this type of publication are La Opinion (The Opinion) of Los Angeles, started in 1926 and its counter-part, La Prensa (The Press) of San Antonio. Nationwide, there are seven Spanish-language dailies in existence today. Such newspapers, even if they had attempted to serve more of a socialization function, would have soon found that they were only communicating with other Spanish-speaking people and not with the entire population. Their specialized audiences prevent Spanish-language papers from serving as an adequate forum for the Spanish-speaking people. And over the years, those concerned with the exclusion of Mexican-Americans from the mainstream of American life have come to the conclusion that the Anglo press has the responsibility of better serving this segment of society.

RACE AND THE MEDIA

Suddenly, with the cause of civil rights at hand, minority leaders found it essential to gain access to the mass media. The movement was in reality a gigantic effort to break into mainstream America, but without being able to communicate with the majority there could be no movement. In order to break down the barriers of bigotry and discrimination, the Southern Negroes and Southwestern Chicanos had to gain the sympathy of the rest of the country—a goal that could not be achieved by the black and Spanish-language media. The nation's system of mass communication had to be utilized, but these minorities found that they had long ago been locked out of the communications industry.

By the early 1960s, the blacks had learned the secret of media coverage and access, as evidenced by the development and refinement of tactics designed to garner the maximum amount of media coverage— the sit-in, the demonstration, the freedom march, and violence. As the Chicano Movement grew, it too benefited from these methods— methods that perhaps would have been unnecessary if these minority groups had sufficient access to the channels of mass communication.

In 1967, during a long hot summer of ghetto riots, President Lyndon B. Johnson appointed Governor Otto Kerner of Illinois to head the National Advisory Commission on Civil Disorders. The Kerner Commission was charged with the task of determining why blacks were rioting in the streets. Its final report placed much of the blame on the mass media:

> The media report and write from the standpoint of a white man's world. The ills of the ghetto, the difficulties of life there, the Negro's burning sense of grievance are seldom conveyed. Slights and indignities are part of the Negro's daily life, and many of them come from what he now calls "the white press"—a press that repeatedly, if unconsciously reflects the biases, the paternalism, the indifference of white America.[7]

The commission argued forcefully that the media alternately ignore and abuse the black minority, allowing the white audience to avoid coming to grips with the problems of the ghetto and their own bigotry. Blacks, the commission said, are afforded little opportunity to make known their grievances and life style, thus perpetuating two separate and unequal communities with no communication between them.

Although the commission does not refer to Mexican-Americans as a minority (a constant source of irritation to leaders of the Chicano Movement) the problems are much the same, if not worse. For the Spanish-speaking person, the problem of intercultural communication is doubled. Not only is he not able to communicate his problems to the English-speaking majority, but he is getting most of his information from a culturally slanted news source. The foreign-language media exist to fill a void that the mass media do not fill; they exist for the unassimilated, those who are not a part of mainstream America. For example, El Diario (The Daily) is a Spanish-language tabloid daily in New York City which serves more than 76,000 readers, making it the largest foreign language publication in the country. A 1968 analysis of the paper revealed the following:

> El Diario showed 50% Latin orientation on its front page, 46% on its "important" news pages, 78% on its inside news space and 75% of its sports space. In addition, El Diario on occasion, added a Latin slant to its coverage of essentially nonethnic news items. . . .
> What this means quite simply is that the Puerto Rican butcher, baker and taxi driver in New York City is reading, more often than not, different news than that read by his New York Daily News-reading counterpart. He, a member of the minority, is not reading much of the news read by the majority of New York City newspaper readers.[8]

The problem is compounded by the lack of minority persons working in news-gathering and editing capacities in the established media. This point was also hit hard by the Kerner Commission as one of the most obvious signs of racism in the media:

The journalistic profession has been shockingly backward in seeking out, hiring, training, and promoting Negroes. Fewer than 5% of the people employed by the news business in editorial jobs in the United States today are Negroes. Fewer than 1% of editors and supervisors are Negroes, and most of them work for Negro-owned organizations. . . . News organizations must employ enough Negroes in positions of significant responsibility to establish an effective link to Negro actions and ideas and to meet legitimate employment expectations.[9]

Available data on employment in the media verify the fact that Spanish-speaking people are also virtually excluded from participating in the nation's system of communication. In 1970, the Community Relations Service (CRS) of the U.S. Department of Justice compiled an unpublished report entitled "Minorities in the Communications Industry." The data were obtained for broadcasting from the Research Department of the Federal Communications Commission (FCC) and for the print media from the Equal Employment Opportunity Commission.[10] The findings support the Kerner Commission assertions.

In the print media, the study sampled the cities in the top 50 media markets. Six of these cities are in areas of the United States with large Spanish-speaking populations, of which most are Mexican-American. These cities are Chicago, Los Angeles, Houston, Dallas, San Francisco-Oakland, and Kansas City. The total number of persons employed in all six cities in the printing and publishing industry was 102,867. Of this number, 10 percent or 10,501 are black and 5 percent or 5,541 are Spanish-speaking. But of those who are Spanish-speaking, only .1 percent or 169 are employed in the two top categories of employment—"official-manager" and "professional." In Los Angeles, the city with the largest percentage of Mexican-Americans of the six, there are 19,512 persons employed in the print media, 2,081 of which are Spanish-speaking. Of this number, only 43 are in the "official-manager" category, while 44 are in the "professional" category. All the rest are in jobs that range from unskilled labor to technical, the bulk (1,534) being employed as blue-collar workers.

A study conducted by the Arizona Journalism Institute in early 1971 attempted to ascertain Mexican-American participation in daily newspapers in the Southwest and in schools of journalism.[11] Questionnaires were sent to 69 daily newspapers in communities that had a

1960 census of 5,000 or more Spanish-surname residents in Arizona, California, Colorado, New Mexico, and Texas. Thirty-seven papers (53 percent) responded and 73 percent of the 41 journalism departments at four-year schools answered the questionnaires. The survey showed that although Spanish-surname residents formed about 14 percent of the population, only 5.6 percent (81 of 1,424) of the news executives, copy editors, reporters, and photographers were of Mexican-American heritage; only 7.5 percent (285 of 3,776) of the journalism students were Mexican-Americans; and none (0 of 165) of the college-level journalism teachers were of Mexican-American heritage.

Broadcasting statistics reflect the same trend. The CRS study gives figures for the three networks and for stations in the top 50 markets, broken down by job categories and by full-time, part-time, and on-the-job training status.

It also includes the data from a study conducted by the National Association of Educational Broadcasters (NAEB) in 1971 on minority employment in public television stations and educational television stations. For the purpose of this discussion, the figures for the three networks, for all PTV and ETV stations and for a sample of four pertinent cities (Chicago, Los Angeles, Houston, and San Francisco-Oakland), were extracted from the data. The total number of full-time employees in all categories for these stations and network headquarters was 27,549. The data show that 7 percent of these are black and 656 or 2.5 percent are Spanish-speaking. Furthermore, the Spanish-speaking total can be broken down by job categories. When this is done, the following totals result:

Stations	"Officials and Managers"	"Professionals"
Networks	26	51
Four Cities	9	34
PTV and ETV	14	120

Thus, although 2.5 percent of the total number of full-time employees are Spanish-speaking, less than 1 percent are in jobs that affect the content of the programming.[12]

The most comprehensive study of minority employment in broadcasting is one completed in November 1972 by the United Church of Christ's Office of Communication.[13] Using the minority employment forms required by the FCC to be filled out by all broadcast stations, the Church of Christ computerized the data and constructed a precise picture of minority hiring practices in the electronic media. For the purposes of this study, the data pertinent to Mexican-Americans were extracted and can be examined quickly in the six tables provided (see

Appendix B). The tables, which show minority hiring nationwide and in each of the five Southwestern states, are further broken down by total number of employees, by number of blacks and of Spanish-surnamed Americans and by job categories. The author computed percentages of minority people employed and extracted the number of Spanish-surnamed people holding jobs that actually allow them to influence programming. In the original survey, there are nine categories of employment: officials and managers, professionals, technicians, sales workers, office and clerical, craftsmen, operatives, laborers, and service workers. The tables here only report the top two categories for Spanish-surnamed persons.

Generally, the data show that blacks and browns lack a significant voice in the electronic commercial media. Only 6.8 percent of the total 39,071 full-time employees nationwide are black and 2.7 percent have Spanish surnames. But the figures are a slight improvement over 1971, at which time they were 5.9 percent and 2.2 percent, respectively. Of the 1,048 Spanish-surnamed employees, 127 are employed as officials or managers and 207 as professionals, meaning that less than 1 percent of the nation's commercial broadcast employees at the policymaking level are of Latin descent.

Of the 3,811 part-time employees, 12.8 percent are black and 4.2 percent are of Latin descent, and of the 781 on-the-job trainees 20.7 percent are black and 21.9 percent are Latin descendants. The percentages in the latter category showed a significant jump for the Spanish-speaking from the previous year, perhaps due to the increasing pressure of the Chicano Movement. Spanish-surnamed on-the-job trainees increased from 3.5 percent in 1971, but dropped from 21 percent for blacks.

At the state level in the Southwest, Texas has the highest percentage of Latins employed full-time, with 8.2 percent (where 18 percent of the population is Mexican-American) and Colorado has the lowest percentage with 4.9 percent (13 percent of this state is of Latin descent). Of the other three states, their percentages of employment and percentages of Spanish-speaking population are: New Mexico, 7.9 percent (40 percent); California, 6.7 percent (16 percent); and Arizona, 6.7 percent (19 percent). The figures for employees in the top two categories of employment reflect the true nature of the statistics. In Texas there are 52 Latins employed in positions that allow them to influence programming; in California there are 86; in Arizona there are 9; in Colorado there are 7; and in New Mexico there are 5.

Despite the dismal situation for Mexican-Americans at present, the comparisons of the two years indicate some improvement, but not enough to predict a trend. In almost all categories for all five states, percentages of employment jumped between one and two percentage points in one year.

Statistics such as these have not been overlooked by the federal machinery set up to insure implementation of the 1964 Civil Rights Act. In March 1969, one of those agencies, the U.S. Equal Employment Opportunity Commission (EEOC), held hearings in Hollywood, California, to determine whether or not it should recommend to the Justice Department that it file suit against the three major television networks for employment discrimination.

The commission had previously recommended such action be taken against the motion picture industry (including all film companies, the Association of Motion Picture and TV Producers, and a number of unions), after a careful examination of the industry's experience-roster system.[14]

During the Hollywood hearings, Clifford L. Alexander, chairman of the commission, heard the three network coast vice presidents defend their policies and contend that they were actively seeking to hire minority workers. Surrounded by other members of the five-man commission, he warned the networks that "TV is going to have to live up to its responsibilities." The networks had promised to end any discrimination at hearings 15 months before in New York City. But Alexander felt the promise had not been kept. He charged that the networks have policies that exclude minorities and asked network officials how TV can accurately cover a Mexican situation involving a Mexican-American who may not speak English, when they don't have representatives of this minority as TV newsmen. He also asked if there were any Mexican-American producers in TV or any Mexican-American agents. The answers to both questions were negative. The commission decided not to ask for a Justice Department suit, but concluded by describing the minority employment picture for the three major radio and TV networks in the L.A. area as "discouraging." He said it was not the raw numbers that counted so much as the fact that the networks play a critical role in influencing public opinion and creating the nation's image of itself: "To portray the country accurately, the industry must hire minority personnel at all levels."

More recently, the FCC has cracked down on job bias in the television industry nationwide.[15] The first black FCC commissioner, Benjamin Hooks, was recently asked by chairman Dean Burch to draw up new FCC criteria for evaluation of the employment practices of licensees. He even went as far as suggesting that what might be needed in the near future was a new organizational office for equal employment within the commission. One of Hooks's first moves in this regard took place in August 1972 when he queried 30 broadcasters in Pennsylvania and Delaware about their minority hiring practices. The stations had reported either no minority group or female employees or a decline in those employee categories from 1971 to 1972. This action was the first real effort to implement the 1970 FCC rules barring discrimination, and it marked what many believe is a long-term push for real enforcement of those rules.

If the employment figures seem discouraging to Mexican-Americans, then ownership and programming statistics must seem devastating to a movement that requires so much communication. There is no general audience newspaper, magazine, radio, or television station owned or managed by a minority group member in the United States today.[16] No black or brown person owns or controls a television station of any kind anywhere in the U.S. Even those papers and broadcast stations that are geared to black or Spanish-speaking audiences are mostly owned by Anglos.

Of approximately 7,000 radio stations in America, 234 carry at least 15 minutes per week of Spanish-language programming, according to the 1972 Broadcasting Yearbook. Only 5.6 percent, or 13 stations out of the 234, broadcast in Spanish 100 percent of the time and 29 carry at least 20 hours per week.[17] By 1972, there were about 60 television stations that carried some Spanish-language advertisements or programming in the United States.[18]

Prospects for future participation of Spanish-speaking persons in the media do not look any brighter. A survey conducted by the National Association of Broadcasters (NAB) in 1972 found that there were only 70 colleges and universities with Spanish-surnamed students taking broadcasting courses.[19] (Actually, the number is less since those schools with graduate programs were counted twice.) The study surveyed 124 four-year schools, 65 of which had graduate programs, and 19 two-year schools, for a total of 208. The total number of students enrolled in broadcasting in all schools was 10,011. Of these, 286 had Spanish surnames (about 2.7 percent). There were 154 attending undergraduate four-year schools, 34 in graduate courses, and 98 at two-year schools.[20]

In the print media, the only available study is the previously mentioned one conducted by the Arizona Journalism Institute in 1971 that found 285 students of Mexican heritage enrolled as journalism students in 41 departments of journalism in the five Southwestern states. This figure was 7.5 percent of the 3,776 students counted. The survey also found that there were no college-level journalism teachers of Mexican-American heritage in the Southwest. Since the study was conducted, however, there have been at least four hired, the author (as the chairman of the department of journalism) and John Siquieros (chairman of the department of broadcasting), both at the University of Texas at El Paso. New Mexico State University and New Mexico Highlands University have also hired at least one Mexican-American each, since the survey was conducted, as journalism instructors.[21]

MEDIA COVERAGE OF MEXICAN-AMERICANS

Until just recently, daily newspapers in this country have given little coverage to the Spanish-speaking community. In the Southwest, Mexican-Americans have been traditionally left out of the news columns except when involved in crimes or accidents. In the society pages, Spanish names simply did not appear unless they were in reference to visiting dignitaries or to the wealthiest Mexican families. In the late 1950s and early 1960s papers began using small pictures of Mexican-American brides on the back page of the society section for the first time, but even then, Anglo marriages were given much larger play. Although there has been no significant research conducted in the area of newspaper coverage of Mexican-Americans, the author has particular insight into the problem because his father was one of the first Mexican-American newsmen in the Southwest. During his years as a reporter for the El Paso Herald-Post in the mid-thirties, Francisco J. Lewels, Sr. observed at first hand the editorial policy of that paper in a city with nearly 50 percent Mexican-American population. He recalls one incident that summarizes what he believes to be the paper's general attitude: a report had just come into the newsroom that there had been a traffic fatality in the city. In order to meet the rapidly approaching deadline, the headline had to be written immediately, and the editor called for a banner headline stretching across the page. Then, as an afterthought, he asked, "Was it a Mex?" The answer was "yes." "Well, then," he said, "better give me a one column head."[22]

Today, in the same city, there is still no regular coverage of the Mexican-American community, no Mexican-American column about local problems nor any news in Spanish. This situation led to a confrontation between Chicanos and the Herald-Post and the El Paso Times, both of which enjoy antitrust immunity under the 1970 Newspaper Preservation Act. They operate joint printing facilities, joint circulation and joint advertising departments, and pool their profits according to circulation.[23] The Times is a morning paper and the Post is an evening paper; neither has any competition.

On September 16, 1972 (Mexican Independence Day) approximately 100 Chicano demonstrators sat on the sidewalk across from the two papers' joint operation while spokesmen for the group attempted to speak with the editors of the two papers to demand a revision of their editorial policies. Ricardo Sanchez, one of the leaders, stated the group's complaints:

> We want to show this newspaper and other newspapers
> that the mass media are very insensitive to the needs of
> the Chicano. We are treated as a minority. In actuality
> we are a majority of El Paso County. We demand more

equal coverage. We demand more Chicanos on ne
staffs, exposes on education, social services and ~
mafias and the inclusion of a regular guest column
Chicano columnists.24

Jose Medina, one of the leaders of the demonstrator
in a personal interview that they were allowed into the bui __, but
that neither of the two editors would see them personally, and that
none of the charges or demands were ever answered in the papers.
There have been no visible changes in the papers since the incident.25

However, the El Paso Times did print a letter to the editor
written by one of the demonstrators a few days after the incident.
The author, Salvador Valdez, elaborated on Chicano media problems:

The local papers have only a few Spanish surnames to add
color to their staff. But these reporters are like worms
inside holes who cannot come out because their heads are
cut off by their racist editors. Therefore, they move in-
effectively underground. Our people in El Paso compose
the biggest amount of subscribers to the local papers and
still in the social pages we are hidden on the least important parts of the papers. Locally, when we make news is
when we show our frustrations against the Anglo institutions which are not serving us adequately. The publicity
always has the smell of racism, and very few articles are
favorable to the Chicano. These few good articles are
overshadowed by big advertisements. Because we do not
have the access that we should with the news media that
we patronize, our people are always kept unaware and
therefore are kept uninformed. When vital issues come
up in which objectivity should be at its best we always
find the papers against us.26

It is safe to say that the same problems exist in other parts of
the Southwest. Another example is Tucson, Arizona, where an almost
identical situation exists in the monopolistic hold of the two daily newspapers. The Arizona Daily Star and the Tucson Daily Citizen have an
identical antitrust exempted agreement and enjoy no other competition.
A survey conducted by Minette "Toby" Burges, editor of the Arizona
Daily Wildcat, found that 65 percent of a sample of Tucson Mexican-
Americans consider themselves ignored by the two daily papers. Of
these, 68 percent said they felt their community was not sufficiently
covered by either paper and 48 percent read both papers regularly.27

In general, she found that Mexican-Americans would like to see
more coverage in Spanish, more stories about the Mexican-American

community itself, including investigations of schools and housing, as well as more Mexican-American reporters, listings of job opportunities free of charge, the creation of a Chicano section, and expanded photographic and reporting coverage. Many of the respondents asked for a change in philosophy and attitude on the part of the downtown newspapers. To rectify the lack of coverage in the community, 35 percent said a newspaper written exclusively for Mexican-Americans should be established to fill the gap and 20 percent asked for expanded coverage by the established press. The 29 Mexican-Americans sampled ranged in age from 20 to 56 and considered themselves to be all the way from far left to far right politically. They came from all socio-economic levels of the community.

But if the media seem unresponsive to the Mexican-American, it may be that the people in the media do not know how to handle the problem of minority coverage even when they try. The Tucson Daily Citizen editors even had a hard time deciding how to refer to Spanish-surname persons in its news columns and finally had to turn the problem over to Adolfo Quezada, a Mexican-American reporter, for his consideration and a staff memo. The problem was whether to refer to them as "Chicano" or "Mexican-American." This was Quezada's reply:

> The Mexican-American community is composed of different types of people with varying backgrounds and experiences in life. What they choose to call themselves is usually a reflection on those experiences. In Tucson, we find that the overwhelming majority of Mexican-Americans consider themselves just that. They are Americans and because they are distinguishable as having a Mexican heritage they are appropriately referred to as Mexican-Americans. One group of younger, energetic, sincere, concerned and, up to now nonmilitant Mexican-Americans chooses to call itself Chicano. The group is small but growing . . . . [28]

From this, the Citizen has formulated the writing and headline policy that "Chicano" is not a correct generic term for all Americans of Mexican heritage, and an attempt is made to distinguish between the two.

In other parts of the United States, print coverage is beginning to increase. Major English-language papers are establishing news summaries and community service columns as regular features in their news pages. Among these columns are the Chicago Tribune's "Accion Rapida," the Philadelphia Daily News's "Entre Col y Col," and the Boston Herald Traveler's "Noticias."[29] As previously

mentioned, one of the most effective and well-respected co
the problems of Mexican-Americans was that of Ruben Sal
was killed while covering riots in Los Angeles. No newsm
come close to replacing him as the leading Mexican-Ameri
nalist.

ELECTRONIC MEDIA COVERAGE

Broadcast coverage and programming for Mexican-Americans
has reflected the communication gap between the two cultures as well
as the ignorance of the Anglo media owner about the Spanish-speaking
segment of his audience and the ignorance of Mexican-Americans
about the mass media. Until the mid-1960s there was very little
interest and very few attempts by the media to reach this audience in
any way. Along the border, it was assumed that Mexican-Americans
listened only to Mexican stations from across the border for news and
information and watched Mexican television for entertainment. But
by 1962, Mexican-Americans were beginning to turn to English-
language stations for entertainment and for whatever local coverage
was available. A study performed in that year, based on a sample of
500 Mexican-American families in 12 of the largest concentrations
of Mexican-American population in the Southwest, disclosed that 88
percent of the households had one or more radios, 87 percent had a
television set, and 72 percent had car radios.[30] It revealed that 78
percent read English-language newspapers, 73 percent read English-
language magazines, and 47 percent attended English-language movies
regularly. But broadcasters did not seem interested in tapping the
market. Only $5 million in advertising was invested in Spanish-
language broadcasting that year.

Broadcasting magazine announced that, by 1966, the Spanish-
speaking consumer market was valued at about $8 billion and that
even though the amount invested in programming for that audience
had more than doubled since 1962, it was still "undersold, under-
bought and undervalued." It added that the "biggest impediment in
the way of Spanish-language advertising is the apparent unwillingness
of many advertisers even to test it."[31] But, slowly, the broadcast
media began to mine the Spanish ore that had for so long been overlooked. By the summer of 1969 there were four television stations
that broadcast solely in Spanish—New York's WXTV, KMEX in Los
Angeles, KWEX in San Antonio, and KPAZ in Phoenix—all UHF. These
four, along with five stations in Mexico, make up the Spanish International Network (SIN), an organization established to exploit the rich
Spanish-language market by providing Spanish programming for its
own and other subscribing stations.[32]

47

SIN gets most of its programming from a huge tape-production center in Mexico City called Telesistema Mexicano, the largest producer of Spanish-language TV programs in the world. The company operates 29 TV stations in Mexico and maintains a production center called Televicentro with 15 studios that telecast 24 hours a day, using 13 videotape machines, 13 remote units, and two color units. Employing 1,500 full-time workers, Telesistema produces 80 live-on-tape shows every week. The shows range from soap operas, musical varieties, folklore to bullfights and special events such as Mexican Independence Day festivities. The most popular of its shows is the telenovela (soap opera) of which it produces 30 half-hour episodes per week—more than 1,500 per year. Mexico's best actors, producers, directors, writers, and designers are brought together for the production of the stories, which command the highest ratings wherever they are shown. In 1969, KMEX-TV found that one of these telenovelas recorded the station's largest viewing audience—an average of 53,400 receivers.[33]

Next in popularity is the musical variety show, produced by telesistema in great quantities—from 40 to 50 half-hour programs per week. They employ singers, dancers, bands, girls, and slapstick comedy to entertain their Spanish-speaking audiences. Sports rank next in popularity and these are provided in the form of bullfights every week from Mexico City and Tijuana, boxing from the capital, wrestling and soccer. A station like KMEX receives 70,000 to 80,000 feet of video tape and film from Mexico every week.

Besides entertainment, Spanish-language audiences get commercials. In 1968, Med-Mark, Inc. was formed to conduct market surveys of UHF-station audiences. It found that even though most viewers with Spanish surnames were bilingual, they strongly preferred Spanish-language broadcasting. Moreover, they were quick to develop a loyalty to advertisers' products (a brand loyalty far exceeding that of Anglo viewers) and they were also more receptive to advertisers' promotional campaigns.[34]

All of this has produced somewhat of a boom in Spanish-language programming in just the last two years or so. But it is a boom that many Mexican-Americans say is doing more harm than good. The complaint is mainly with the type of programming. Broadcasters, they claimed, find it too easy to use canned tapes and films that come from Mexico. These, they say, do not reflect Mexican-American life and do more to perpetuate isolationism than anything else. There is also a tendency to avoid community programs and to succumb to the temptation of doing "rip and read" (from the teletype) newscasting, rather than spending money on reporters.

Fidel Gonzalez, California director of the League of United Latin-American Citizens (LULAC) sees Spanish-language programming

as a "barren wasteland . . . burdened with substandard programing,
blaring announcements, and a general apathy to their [the stations]
own community."[35] Pete Rodriquez, working with the Experimental
System for Education's Community Media Complex in Los Angeles,
believes that although Spanish broadcasting serves a valuable purpose,
it also perpetuates isolationism within the community. He suggests
bilingual broadcasting as a better solution to the problem of intercultural communication.

But others have hope for the new surge in programming. Danny
Villanueva, KMEX-TV vice president and general manager, sees his
station as a visible force in the community. The station's gross bill-
ings have jumped 450 percent in two years, to a projected $3 million
in 1972, thereby financing expanded community operations. Villanueva
has dreams of a fourth TV network; eventually covering 95 percent of
the nation as "a voice of the people." But, such dreams are far from
being fulfilled. Few stations are actually doing much in the way of
educational, informative community programming that would be bene-
ficial in helping Mexican-Americans assimilate and function in society.
However, there are some examples of efforts to program for the
social good. One radio station that has tried in Southern California
is XEGM-AM, with studios in Hollywood but transmissions beamed
from Mexico. The station carries an open-forum program for community use, but Elias Liberman, a station executive, is dismayed by
the apathy and a general reluctance of responsible community leaders
to use the facilities available to them. He says the station barely got
a nibble from an offer of free announcements, aid, and air time to
responsible community groups.[36]

The same problem has been found in other areas of the country
where Spanish-speaking people have been excluded for so long from
participating in the media that when they are given the chance they do
not understand the significance or the procedure for doing so. Station
KWKW-AM in Los Angeles, which has been programming entirely in
Spanish since 1956, however, has had success with its community-
affairs program called Tribunal Libre (Free Tribunal). The show is
an open forum that attracts community leaders who enter into a two-
way radio format.[37]

One of the best examples of what can be done began in 1969 with
a Ford Foundation grant to KLRN-TV, an English-language educational
station in San Antonio. The station, faced with a severe gap in intercultural communication, initiated its program for and by the Mexican-
American. Although Spanish is the language of presentation, 80 percent of the time on the show, English is used when necessary. The
program entitled Periodico (Newspaper) was started with the under-
lying philosophy that Mexican-Americans have a beautiful heritage
and they should be proud. In attempting to underline this heritage in

production, the show carries lessons related to Mexican-American
ributions not only to their own history, but to the total history of
e nation and the area. There are performances by Mexican-American
artists, dancers, actors, and musicians, as well as displays of Mexican-
American paintings and sculpture. There are "how to do it" segments
that range from how to stretch the family budget and assure good
nutrition to how to train for available careers (accenting success
stories from the neighborhood).[38]

One of the biggest problems facing community affairs programming
for the Spanish-speaking is the unwillingness of broadcasters to spend
the money necessary and provide the time for such programs. Until
the Chicano Movement began, most of the funding for such programming
came from foundations which made grants to public or educational
broadcast stations. Programming of this type instigated in the past
two years that is not a result of the movement could well be due to
the FCC's prime-time access rule, which was not really intended to
increase the amount of prime time devoted to news and public affairs
programming. However, a 1972 study shows that this was indeed the
case. The rule provided an ideal opportunity for local stations to use
vacated prime time to meet local public-service responsibilities by
expanding news coverage and public-affairs programming. Of the 95
stations responding to the survey, 17 indicated that they would increase
locally produced news shows by at least one-half hour per week. Another 34 stations reported they would increase locally produced public
affairs programs by a half hour per week or more.[39]

MASS MEDIA AND THE PROBLEM
OF STEREOTYPE

The face of the mayor of San Antonio, W. W. McAlister, was
being viewed in living color by millions of Americans across the
country on July 6, 1970, during an interview on the Huntley-Brinkley
Report, when he launched into his concept of the Mexican-American
character:

> You have to bear in mind that there is a special tempera-
> ment . . . a difference of temperament between the
> Anglos and our Americans of Mexican descent. Our citi-
> zens of Mexican descent are very fine people . . . uh . . .
> they're . . . they're home loving . . . they love beauty
> . . . they love flowers . . . they love music-ah-they love
> dancing . . . uh . . . perhaps they're not quite as let's
> say as ambitiously motivated as the Anglos are to get
> ahead financially, but they manage to get a lot out of
> life.[40]

50

Understandably, many Mexican-Americans became enraged by what seemed to them the stupidity and naïveté of the stereotyped image that he painted. To have such utterances come from the mayor of one of the most predominantly Mexican-American cities in the nation was even more devastating. For what Mayor McAlister did, Mexican-Americans knew, was simply to state before the entire country the attitude of most Southwestern Anglos toward their Spanish-speaking neighbors. The fact that he did it on national television, they felt, just served to spread and perpetuate the myth of white racial supremacy that such stereotypes evoke.

Because the problem of stereotyping has been a prime target of the Chicano Movement, it is important to understand not only how the media perpetuate stereotypes, but what stereotypes are and what social functions they serve. Only then can the media and minority groups come to terms with the problem that seems destined to be around for as long as there are media and people to consume their products.

Sociologist Gordon Allport gives this definition of a stereotype:

> A stereotype is an exaggerated belief associated with a category, and its function is to justify conduct in relation to that category.

Allport believes that people use stereotypes to rationalize their own weaknesses and failures:

> Suppose there are unwanted traits in oneself—perhaps greed, lust, laziness and untidiness. What the sufferer needs is a caricature of these attributes—a simon pure incarnation of these evils. He needs something so extreme that he need not even suspect himself of being guilty. The Jew is therefore seen as wholly concupiscent; the Negro as completely lazy; the Mexican as filthy. One who holds such extreme stereotypes need not suspect himself of having these hated tendencies.[41]

In creating stereotypes, people are essentially simplifying the world around them. Walter Lippmann believes that it is a matter of forming habits of simple apprehension in order to introduce (1) definiteness and distinction and (2) consistency or stability of meaning into what is otherwise vague and wavering.[42] Thus, stereotyping is a natural human process common to all people and, according to Lippmann, it is a process that involves not only our moral codes, social philosophies, and political agitations, but also the manner in which images are presented through art, literature, and the media.

The problem occurs because people are not aware of their stereotypes and therefore treat them seriously. Instead of realizing that man's "intelligence catches at best only phases and aspects in a course net of ideas," and instead of being ready to modify stereotypes, people tend to cling to them and to codify the world according to their own individual code.[43]

So, due to natural human failures, the media can easily serve to perpetuate stereotypes by presenting those of the communicators and by intentionally catering to those of the mass audience. Those who wish to censor the media probably do not underestimate its influence, according to Lippmann, but rather misunderstand it. Lippmann compares such people to Plato, who felt vaguely that the poets of his time created types which tended to be imposed on reality by the audience. Today, he says, the motion picture is even more powerful in this respect:

> Thus, there can be little doubt that the moving picture is steadily building up imagery which is then evoked by the words people read in their newspapers. In the whole experience of the race there has been no aid to visualization comparable to the cinema. . . . Photographs have the kind of authority over imagination today, which the printed word had yesterday and the spoken word before that. They seem utterly real. They come, we imagine, directly to us without human meddling, and they are the most effortless food for the mind conceivable. . . . The shadowy idea becomes vivid: your hazy notion, let us say, of the Ku Klux Klan . . . takes vivid shape when you see the Birth of a Nation. Historically, it may be the wrong shape, morally it may be a pernicious shape, but it is a shape, and I doubt whether anyone who has seen the film . . . will ever hear the name again without seeing those white horsemen.[44]

Numerous psychological and sociological studies have treated ethnic and racial stereotypes as they appear publicly in the mass media and also as held by individuals. Some of these have concentrated on Mexican-Americans and have resulted in similar findings.[45] A study by Ozzie G. Simmons[46] describes the Anglo stereotype of Mexican-Americans. He found that Anglo-Americans believe that the assimilation of Mexican-Americans is only a matter of time, contingent solely on the full incorporation of Anglo-American values and ways of life. (This, of course, is what the Chicano Movement is fighting.) Anglos also tend to categorize Mexican-Americans into two distinct classes: the "high type" and the "low type." This is based on three criteria: occupational achievement and wealth (the Anglo's own principal criteria of status) and command of Anglo-American ways. The "high type" people are acceptable for membership in the service clubs and can intermarry, but are not necessarily fully accepted. Simmons also found that Anglos have a contrasting belief that Mexican-Americans are essentially inferior. The same people expressed both assumptions at different times and in different situations.

It is the presumption of inferiority that Simmons sees as the basis for rationalization in Allport's definition. He believes that Anglos in the Southwest use the stereotype of Mexican-American inferiority to rationalize their subordinate status as "being their own fault." They are ready to identify Mexican-Americans with menial labor and to buttress their Anglo image with beliefs that Mexican-Americans are improvident, undependable, irresponsible, childlike, and indolent. Therefore, they rationalize, if Mexicans are fit for only the humblest labor, there is nothing abnormal about the fact that most Mexican workers are at the bottom of the occupational pyramid, and the fact that most Mexicans are unskilled workers is sufficient proof that they belong in that category. Associated with these beliefs is the image of homogeneity. Even though they are classified as being of "low" and "high" types, Mexican-Americans are thought of as being essentially the same: "a Mexican is a Mexican." Either image serves a purpose according to the situation. The assumption that all Mexicans are alike buttresses the assumption of inferiority by making it convenient to ignore the fact of the existence of a substantial number of Mexican-Americans who represent all levels of business and professional achievement. Such people, they rationalize, are exceptions to the rule.[47]

Other commonly held beliefs are that Mexicans are unclean, they tend toward drunkenness and criminality, and they are deceitful and of low morality. Simmons points out that the belief that they are unclean justifies avoiding social contact and exclusion from swimming pools and other recreation facilities. The other assumptions justify blanket exclusion from full participation in activities of the community.

Thus, the power of the media becomes quite clear to the leaders of the social movement seeking relief from discrimination and the hardships of inferior education, poor housing, and low-paying jobs that accompany it. The mass media were immediately fingered as being the fastest means of affecting change in stereotypes as well as for being their most fervent manipulators. Soon, the issue of identity and stereotype became the major issue of a great deal of political activity within the Chicano Movement, which, for the first time, confronted the cultural and racial stereotypes held by the Anglos. Like the blacks who revolted against their "Amos and Andy" and "Stepin

Fetchit" image, Chicanos began a concentrated attack on the media that portrayed them as being lazy, shiftless, gun-toting, guitar-playing, and peasantlike.

WHO KILLED JOSE JIMENEZ?

The anger and frustration of the Chicano activist is vented by Armando Rendon in The Chicano Manifesto:

> . . . the Anglo has had tremendous opportunity to exploit
> and perpetuate the caricature Chicano. With control
> over the media, the Anglo has been able to keep alive
> the false front of the lazy Mexicano.[48]

He believes that one of the most tragic effects of media stereotyping is the absence of a positive image of the Mexican-American for Chicano youths to imitate. He asks: "How do you undo the harm of one Frito Bandito commercial or the adverse effects of an ad showing a single Anglo, gun in hand, in control of three swarthy-looking Mexican-Americans?" Rendon also believes that Chicanos are being made the communication industry's "new nigger": "Since they can no longer denigrate the Negro, they turn to safer prey such as the Chicano and the Indian."[49]

One who documented Mexican-American stereotyping in commercial advertising is Dr. Thomas Martinez, director of seminars on Mexican-Americans at Stanford University. This is what he concluded:

> TV commercials and magazine advertisements . . .
> symbolically reaffirm the inferior status of Mexicans and
> Mexican-Americans in the eyes of the audience. Ex-
> aggerated Mexican racial and cultural characteristics,
> together with some outright misconceptions concerning
> their way of life, symbolically suggest to the audience
> that such people are comical, lazy, and thieving, who
> want what the Anglos can have by virtue of their superior
> taste and culture. The advertisements suggest to the
> audience that one ought to buy the produce because it is
> the duty of a member of a superior culture and race.[50]

Martinez cites many examples of racist advertising. One that makes Mexican-Americans cringe with near horror was produced for Arid deodorant. The commercial begins with a band of ferocious-looking Mexican banditos emerging from a cloud of dust on horseback.

54

They are called to a halt by their sombrero-covered, thick-mustachioed, fat-bellied leader, who, upon stopping, reaches into his saddle bag and retrieves a can of Arid. He lifts up his underarm, smiles slyly, and sprays. An American-Anglo voice is then heard to say, "If it works for him, it will work for you!" The message is obvious: Mexicans stink more than other people.

Another blatant example of media insensitivity to the feelings of Mexican-Americans was the May 1970 newspaper campaign by Elgin National Industries, which used an ad that announced: "Your new Elgin is better than the Elgins Zapata was willing to kill for in 1914." It concluded, "It's a good thing Emiliano Zapata's gone. He'd be stealing Elgins as fast as we could make them." Obviously, the ad agency was ignorant of the fact that Zapata is considered a national hero in Mexico and by Mexican-Americans—not a bandit.

Such insensitivity to Mexican-Americans, Chicano leaders feel, must be corrected. Rendon and Domingo Nick Reyes, testifying before the Senate Equal Educational Opportunity Committee in 1970 blamed the mass media for not trying to correct the problem:

> The persons who now control the most pervasive means
> of communication are personally at fault for the evil
> consequences of past discrimination and ignorance be-
> cause they have not acted to make amends. Indeed, they
> perpetuate the exploitative and exclusionary practices of
> their predecessors.
>
> Mexican-Americans understand full well what the
> mass media have failed to do for them and what they have
> suffered as a result. They can see themselves as the
> victims of the John Waynes and the Wild Bunches. They
> see themselves denigrated on television, in newspapers,
> and in magazines as banditos, thieves, lazy no-accounts.
> They seldom, if ever, see the names of other Chicanos
> or raza on television or film credits, as by-lines in
> magazine and newspaper articles, or as authors on book
> jackets. They know that the masters of the media exclude
> them, that most likely there is not a thought in their minds
> for the predicament of the Spanish-speaking person.[51]

Determined to change the stereotype of Mexican-Americans to a more positive one, Chicano leaders began their attack on the media in 1968, demanding that reparation be made for the exploitation their people have suffered. Two incidents took place within a week of each other in September 1968 that signaled the launching of a loosely organized attack on the media by the Chicano Movement. The first was the formation of the National Mexican-American Anti-Defamation

55

Committee (NMAADC) in Washington, D.C., by Domingo Nick Reyes.52 Its purpose was to contact advertisers and ad agencies, organize a Washington lobby, create a "talent bank" and organize product boycotts when necessary. Although the committee had operated as a loose confederation of several organizations under the name La Raza Unida, this was the first formal organization set up with the primary purpose of dealing with racial matters in the media.

The organization was specifically formed to combat media stereo-typing of Mexican-Americans by Liggett and Myers in Cigarette ads, Frito-Lay cornchip ads, American Telephone and Telegraph Company ads in which Bill Dana was used as Jose Jimenez, American Motors Corporation ads for Javelins, and Granny Goose potato chip ads. The committee sent letters to these companies protesting in behalf of all Mexican-Americans.

The formation of the committee was announced by Reyes, who at the time was a staff member of the U.S. Commission on Civil Rights and would act as chairman in his spare time. He announced a multistep program for the committee:

1. To urge Mexican-Americans and persons with Spanish surnames not to buy those products which show their minority in a "demeaning and degrading" manner in the mass media.

2. To begin an intensive program of monitoring the mass media for those degrading characterizations and to make the monitoring results known to Mexican-Americans in order to show the extent of discrimination when suggesting buyer boycotts.

3. To continue to write letters to industry and government—including Congress—urging that the focus of mass media be changed so that use of the demeaning stereotypes will be discontinued.

4. To develop a "talent" or "skills" bank—a pool of Mexican-American and Spanish-surname individuals with particular talents who will be available for employment by the media.

Other goals of the committee are to organize a Mexican-American and Spanish-surname lobby in Washington and to promote funding of research projects by government, industry, and foundations to examine the extent of damage to Mexican-Americans and other minorities by mass media stereotyping.

The committee appealed to foundations and other philanthropic institutions for funds and resource people to help in the development of a more positive image for Mexican-Americans and Spanish-surname people.

A week after the formation of the committee, on September 25, the Mexican-American Political Association (MAPA) threatened a boycott of American motion pictures in Mexico and Latin-America if the motion picture and TV producers failed to meet demands that Latins receive equal opportunities in the production industry. Ray Martell, a Mexican-American actor, explained that the goal was to "acquire equal opportunity for all Latins, be they actors, cameramen, or whatever. . . . We want dignified roles for Latin actors, a better and true image—not the stereotyped image of Latins. When there is a sizable or dignified role it goes to any other ethnic group." Martell was disturbed because many Negroes had been getting Latin-American roles. He felt that Mexican-Americans had been victimized by the campaign to hire more Negroes and by the virtual exclusion of Mexican-Americans in positive roles.

> It's astounding that in the history of movies and tv that
> there has yet to be a Latin actor who has a leading role
> in a cowboy series, when the very idea of cowboys
> originated with the Spaniards and Mexicans.[53]

With the threat of the boycott in Hollywood and the formation of the Anti-Defamation Committee in Washington, the communications industry received its first warning that Mexican-Americans were serious about making substantial reforms. With this warning, the attack against media stereotypes began. The following month a Mexican-American group in San Antonio called Involvement of Mexican-Americans in Gainful Endeavor (IMAGE) took Bill Dana's Jose Jimenez show to task for perpetuating the image of Latin-Americans as "serape-draped, wall-leaning sun-dozers."[54] Dana responded by forming his own organization, Latin-Americans in United Direction (LAUD) to push for more recognition and representation for Mexican-Americans. The group's first project was a 90 minute television program in Los Angeles featuring Mexican-Americans. But the effort was not enough to convince the growing number of media groups that the show should stay on the air.

On April 4, 1970, after nearly two years of battle with Chicano media groups, Bill Dana announced to 10,000 cheering Mexican-Americans, at a fete sponsored by the Congress on Mexican-American Unity, that Jose Jimenez was "dead."[55] Meanwhile, another group was busy monitoring the media for more evidence of stereotyping. Professor Martinez of Stanford formed the Council to Advance and Restore the Image of the Spanish-Speaking and Mexican-Americans (CARISSMA) to make complaints to congressmen and corporations when abuses were found.[56] They joined forces with NMAADC and other groups to fight what they felt to be racist advertising and

programming. One of the first victories came in March 1970 when
Frito-Lay agreed to drop the successful Frito-Bandito ads from
television (although today they continue to run in parts of the country
where Mexican-American population is low).

The next battle against the stereotypes began three months later
when the Elgin Company ran their newspaper ad portraying the Mexican revolutionary hero Emiliano Zapata as a thief. The first paper
to carry the advertisement was the Chicago Tribune. Mike Royko,
Chicago Daily News columnist describes the reaction of the Mexican-
American community of that city:

> Mexicans in Chicago were stunned. Since Zapata is one
> of their national heroes, they couldn't believe that any-
> body would be so coarse as to distort history to sell
> timepieces. One of the local Mexican leaders phoned a
> vice-president of Elgin and protested. According to Dr.
> Jorge Prieto, the conversation went like this: "We
> thought the ad was cute," the vice president said. "What
> the hell do you mean by cute?" the Mexican said. "We
> think it is rather funny," the vice president said.[57]

Next, a march on the Tribune by several hundred Mexican-Americans
was organized. Some of them were able to meet with the paper's
advertising chief, who told them that he had never even heard of
Zapata and then told the leaders of the group that some of his best
friends were Mexican. But despite his friendship with Mexicans, he
did not guarantee the group that he would stop running the ad. A
second march on the Chicago Sun-Times was canceled when Elgin
announced that it was withdrawing the national ad campaign. "Believe
me," an Elgin vice-president said, "it was not our intention to offend
the Mexican community, and we didn't know it would offend them."
To this statement, Royko quipped, "One has to wonder if he would
have been so blithely unaware of the offensiveness of the ad if it had
shown, say, Ben Gurion ordering Arabs shot if they didn't wear Elgin
watches. . . . "

In early 1971, the Anti-Defamation Committee appealed to the
National Association of Broadcasters (NAB) to revise their codes to
protect Mexican-Americans from abusive stereotyping.[58] Reyes
accused the NAB of failing to abide by its own codes, which say that
"Racial or nationality types shall not be shown on television in such
a manner as to ridicule the race or nationality." (NAB TV Code,
Section IV-4). He called for the establishment of a code of conduct
toward the Spanish-speaking people of the U.S., an examination of the
media's current fare of programs, ads, news, and feature coverage
in order to weed out material injurious to the Spanish-speaking, the

establishment of a continuing policy to assure future presentation of positive images, more recruiting and hiring of the Spanish-speaking at all levels in the media, more prime-time allocations for Chicano news and views, and an effort by the electronic media to tell the story of Spanish-speaking Americans through in-depth documentaries.

But even as these demands were being made, old problems were cropping up again for the Committee. Nearly a year after Frito-Lay had promised to remove the gun-toting Frito Bandito from the air, the mustachioed little cartoon character was still riding the airwaves.[59] Joseph L. Gibson, general counsel for the Anti-Defamation Committee announced on January 1, 1971 that the committee would file a lawsuit against the company asking for $610 million in behalf of all demeaned Mexican-American. After the initial furor the year before, NBC and several western television stations declined the Frito Bandito ads, but he still appeared on the other two networks and many Eastern stations. Targets of the suit are Frito-Lay, Foote, Cone and Belding advertising agency, ABC, and CBS. The issue has still not been settled.

By June of 1971, yet another Mexican-American group became involved in the stereotype fight. The group, called Justicia (Justice), met with representatives of the ABC television network and of KABC-TV (the network affiliate in Los Angeles) and announced that they would challenge the license of KABC and KTOP-TV later that year if they did not stop airing certain programs that were considered demeaning to Mexican-Americans.[60] The shows were "The Smith Family," "Alias Smith and Jones," and "Lancelot Link, Secret Chimp." Paul Macias, vice-president of Justicia, said that "These shows portray Mexicans as overly meek, consider us recent transplants from Mexico, cast us as hat-in-hand types, give us mascot roles and generally find us the target of a white hero." Justicia asked for contractual agreements with ABC in five areas: (1) that shows considered demeaning to Chicanos be dropped from the air; (2) that the Frito Bandito commercial be removed from the broadcast schedule; (3) that Justicia be permitted to monitor all scripts which include Spanish-speaking groups and to screen completed programs to insure against demeaning portrayals of Chicanos; (4) that KABC-TV hire a man approved by the Chicanos as its community-relations director; and (5) that the network set aside $10 million in program development funds for shows that feature Chicanos in significant roles in order to restore an image of dignity. Although no formal contract has been reached, there have been advances made in the form of dialogue between the media and Mexican-Americans that never existed before. Justicia had already begun working with CBS network's program-practices division by monitoring programs, but with no veto power. This arrangement seemed to satisfy both sides of the conflict.

Two months later, in August 1971, Justicia blasted NBC for its "Nichols" series.61 Justicia president Ray Andrade threatened a boycott of Chevrolet, the sponsor of the series, if they did not receive a written guarantee that all segments of the series would "properly portray the Chicano with dignity, and [present] Chicanos . . . as contributing to the history of the Southwest." NBC-TV president Don Durgin replied that "NBC portrays Mexican-Americans in a dignified and accurate manner," and that "the network will present nothing it feels is demeaning to them as individuals or as a group. To attempt to contour entertainment programs around ethnic concepts is not only self-defeating but contrary to the justice you seek." He pointed out that the network's West Coast executives had met with Chicano groups a number of times to work out satisfactory agreements and with producers to stress the importance of making opportunities for minority groups and to ensure that they are depicted in terms accurately reflecting their role in American life.

Most of these encounters with the media, even if they did not result in immediate settlement of the problems involved, led the way for a multitude of other groups which saw the possibility of success in challenging their own local media. The publicity generated by these first efforts also made others realize the importance of the media in the everyday affairs of Mexican-Americans and in the total efforts of the civil rights movements. This increased interest nationwide, caused government agencies and private foundations to sponsor well-attended and informative media conferences for Mexican-Americans which resulted in the formation of other, local media organizations, whose goals were to establish dialogue with the media in their communities. The fight against the stereotype, although still an important part of the media movement, has taken a back seat in the past year to goals of employment, training, and in-depth coverage of community problems concerning Mexican-Americans. The result has been astonishingly productive for Chicanos, with the FCC being inundated with license challenges and with broadcast stations taking the brunt of the movement that has concentrated on the point of least resistance. Today, most major cities in the Southwest have at least one broadcast station that has succumbed to the minority pressures and signed far-reaching agreements with Chicano groups that show promise of being positive means of establishing meaningful dialogue.

NOTES

1. John Tebbel, The Complete History of the American Newspaper (New York: Hawthorn Books, Inc., 1969), p. 80.
  2. "First Chicano Press," Somos Aztlan, January 1971, p. 13.

3. Leonard Pitt, The Decline of the Californios (Berkeley, Calif.: University of California Press, 1970), p. 180.

4. Ibid., pp. 181-94.

5. Ibid., p. 194.

6. Edward Moreno, "Mass Media and the Chicano Community" (unpublished paper by Mr. Moreno, an employee of KCET-TV, Los Angeles, July 1970), pp. 3-4.

7. Report of the National Advisory Commission on Civil Disorders (New York: Bantam Books, Inc., 1968), p. 366.

8. David Sacksman, "Two New York Newspapers" (unpublished paper, Stanford University, 1968), p. 11.

9. Report of the National Advisory Commission, p. 369.

10. U. S. Department of Justice, Community Relations Service, "Minorities in the Communications Industry," Washington, D.C., 1971, pp. 24-36. Mimeographed.

11. "Survey of Mexican-Americans in Journalism," Arizona Journalist, September 1971, p. 4.

12. U.S. Department of Justice, "Minorities in the Communications Industry," p. 37.

13. United Church of Christ, Minority Employment Survey of Commercial Television, 1972. (The author obtained the computer printout from the church's office of communication prior to publication of the data.)

14. Dave Kaufman, "U.S. Equal Opportunity Commission Puts Network TV Coast Execs on Hot Seat Re Jobs for Minorities," Variety, March 19, 1969, p. 26.

15. "FCC Crackdown on Job Bias," Variety, August 2, 1972, p. 33.

16. U.S. Department of Justice, Community Relations Service, "CRS Communication Program," Washington, D.C., June 25, 1970, p. 1. Mimeographed.

17. Arturo Barrera, "First National Spanish-Speaking Radio Broadcasting Seminar" (paper delivered at the First National Spanish-Speaking Radio Broadcasting Seminar, Washington, D.C., August 9, 1972), p. 2.

18. Frank Levine, "Spanish-Lingo Broadcasting Booms, with Visions of a 'Fourth Network,' but Barrios Still to Be Hurdled," Variety, August 9, 1972, p. 35.

19. Harold Niven, Colleges and Universities with Minority Group Students Studying Broadcasting (National Association of Broadcasters, 1972), p. 14.

20. Ibid., pp. 15-16.

21. Harvey Jacobs, chairman, Department of Mass Communication, New Mexico State University, private interview held in El Paso, Tex., November 7, 1972 and Ray Newton, chairman, Department of Mass Communication, New Mexico Highlands University, telephone interview, November 15, 1972.

22. Francisco J. Lewels, Sr., private interview held in El Paso, Tex., November 10, 1972.

23. Joe Lewels, Jr., "The Newspaper Preservation Act," Freedom of Information Center Report No. 254 (January 1971), p. 1.

24. El Paso Times, September 16, 1972.

25. Jose Medina, private interview held in El Paso, Tex., November 21, 1972.

26. El Paso Times, letter to the editor, September 21, 1972.

27. Toby Burges, "Report of a Poll of Mexican-Americans," Arizona Journalist, September 1971, p. 4.

28. "Chicano," Arizona Journalist, September 1971, p. 5.

29. "Notices," Forum, April 29, 1972, p. 3. (Forum is a mimeographed newsletter of the U.S. Dept. of Justice, Community Relations Service.)

30. Belden Associates, "The Mexican-American Market in the U.S." (This is a private, unpublished study conducted by Belden Associates in Dallas, Tex. 1962), pp. 1-5.

31. "Spanish Market: Undersold, Undervalued," Broadcasting, September 19, 1966, p. 67.

32. John Tebbel, "Newest TV Boom: Spanish-Language Stations," Saturday Review, June 8, 1969, p. 24.

33. Ibid., p. 25.

34. Ibid., p. 24.

35. Levine, "Spanish-Lingo Broadcasting Booms," p. 35.

36. Ibid.

37. Ibid.

38. Frank Duane, "A People and a Program," Broadcasting and Social Action (Washington, D.C.: National Association of Broadcasters, November 1969), pp. 33-35.

39. Noel L. Griese, "Effects of the FCC's Prime-Time Access Rule on a National Sample of Network Television Stations" (paper presented at the Association for Education in Journalism Annual Convention, Carbondale, Ill., August 21, 1972), p. 12.

40. Jack Perkins, "San Antonio, Part One," The Huntley-Brinkley Report, National Broadcasting Company, aired July 6, 1970.

41. Gordon Allport, The Nature of Prejudice (Cambridge: Addison-Wesley, 1954), p. 191.

42. Walter Lippmann, Public Opinion (New York: Harcourt, Brace & Co., 1922), p. 3.

43. Ibid., p. 7.

44. Ibid., pp. 7-8.

45. Ruth D. Tuck, Not with the Fist (New York: Harcourt, Brace & Co., 1946); Eugene S. Richards, "Attitudes of College Students in the Southwest toward Ethnic Groups in the U.S.," Sociology and Social Research, XXXV (September-October 1950), pp. 22-30; Ed

McDonagh and Eugene S. Richards, Ethnic Relations in the U.S. (New York: Appleton, 1953); John H. Burma, Spanish-Speaking Groups in the United States (Durham, N.C.: Duke University Press, 1954).

46. Ozzie G. Simmons, "The Mutual Images and Expectations of Anglo-Americans and Mexican-Americans," Mexican-Americans in the United States, ed. by John H. Burma (Cambridge, Mass.: Canfield Press, 1970), pp. 383-95.

47. Ibid., p. 386.

48. Armando Rendon, The Chicano Manifesto (New York: Macmillan Co., 1971), p. 48.

49. Ibid., p. 57.

50. Thomas Martinez, "How Advertisers Promote Racism," Civil Rights Digest, Fall 1969, p. 7.

51. U.S. Congress, Senate Committee on Equal Opportunity, Hearings on Equal Education Opportunity before the Select Committee on Equal Opportunity of the U.S. Senate, statement by Domingo Nick Reyes and Armando Rendon, 91st Cong., 1st sess., 1970 (Washington, D.C.: U.S. Government Printing Office, 1970, p. 928 AR.

52. "Anti-Defamation Group Fights Ads Using Spanish Name Stereotypes," Advertising Age, September 30, 1968, p. 94.

53. Dave Kaufman, "2-Mil. Mexicans Can't be Conned, Says Martell; Also-Angry Negro Actors Copping Latin Roles," Variety, September 25, 1968, p. 52.

54. "As We See It," TV Guide, October 5, 1968, p. 28.

55. Los Angeles Times, April 6, 1970.

56. "Mexicans' Defenders Err," Advertising Age, March 16, 1970, p. 32.

57. Chicago Daily News, June 9, 1970.

58. National Association of Broadcasters, TV and Radio Codes, Section IV-4, 1971.

59. Kansas City Star, January 1, 1971.

60. "Chicano's Question: What about Us?" Broadcasting, June 28, 1971, p. 23.

61. "NBC Answers Chicano Beefs on Portrayals," Variety, August 4, 1971, p. 2.

3

THE CHICANO MEDIA MOVEMENT

Grassroots activity in media projects among Chicano groups actually began with the farm worker's movement, as was seen in Chapter 1. The need for access to the channels of communication taught the movement's leaders the value of the media, not only in the labor dispute, but in all areas of the civil rights movement. This new awareness spread throughout the movement rapidly, manifesting itself in a flurry of organizations designed to alter the Mexican-American stereotype through dialogue with media owners and advertisers, and this in turn had the effect of focusing attention on the media as a primary objective. The need to communicate was so great that many groups previously designed for other purposes took on the task of media access and communication as one of their primary goals, and other groups organized for this sole purpose. Almost inevitably, the first efforts in this direction were the production of newspapers, which was seen as the most practical way to gain access to the nationwide press and to tell it to the local community "like it really was."

THE NEW CHICANO PRESS

Chicano newspapers and newsletters, of which at least 50 have sprung up since El Malcriado (their forefather) began telling of the plight of the farm workers, are distinct from the Spanish-language media discussed in Chapter 2. The latter are sedate in comparison to the political activism displayed by such papers as La Revolucion (The Revolution), La Causa, Coraje (Anger), and El Grito (The Cry). About half of these papers are members of the loosely organized Chicano Press Association (CPA), established in the mid-1960s, representing the emergence of a new facet in the broad spectrum of the American press system. The common goal of the CPA was a determination to serve as the voice of the merging Mexican-American civil rights movement.[1] The members agreed to share articles and features with each other and opened membership to "all other publications, committed to improve the news media in the Spanish-speaking community." They also vowed to "improve communication between our people."[2]

According to Frank del Olmo, staff writer for the Los Angeles Times who traveled throughout the Southwest studying the new Chicano newspapers, there are more than 25 members of the CPA, with at least another 25 similar publications not affiliated with the organization.[3] Perhaps because El Malcriado was born in Southern California, this area became the breeding ground for the first of the new breed of papers. In 1967, an underground paper called La Raza was founded in Los Angeles and shortly it had many imitators.[4] At least eight others sprang up in the area, published by such groups as Mexican-American law students, the Barrio Defense Committee (a police watchdog group), and a group of UCLA students. Quickly, the trend spread into other parts of California and into New Mexico, Arizona, Texas, and as far away as Wautoma, Wisconsin, Chicago, and parts of Florida. Among their common traits are their lack of objectivity, their bilingual format, spiced with contemporary poetry and plenty of artwork, their lack of advertising, and their need for funding.

These papers make no pretense at being objective. They believe in being committed to the movimiento and have no qualms about admitting that "sometimes every story we print is an editorial." Among the most politically active are the previously mentioned La Raza; El Grito del Norte, published in Espanola, New Mexico; La Verdad, in San Diego; El Gallo, published by the Crusade for Justice in Denver; and Oakland's Basta Ya![5] In content they are also similar. Most opposed the draft and the Vietnam war (where they saw Chicano casualties as disproportionate to their number in the population). They editorialize against police brutality and for prison reform.[6]

As for their financial status, most editors do not seem overly concerned. Joe Razo, a member of La Raza's editorial board, explained that the paper was not a business venture. "It is an organizational tool. Our aim is not to make money, but to organize our people." For the most part, such papers get support in the form of donations from sympathetic supporters of the organizations they publicize.[7]

Why the papers got started in the first place was a question that del Olmo posed to the various editors. A staff member of El Malcriado explained that "The huelga here in Delano turned on the younger generation. And offset printing enables a small group to put out a paper with little capital or equipment." Another CPA member simply said that they were "trying to fill a gap." Elaborating further, del Olmo explained that "Our people have had few chances to read about themselves because the regular press carries little about them. . . . There is a renaissance going on in the barrios that these papers are the start of."[8]

THE NEW RENAISSANCE

But if it was the new, militant Chicano press that was to start the new renaissance, then it was the Citizen Action Group (CAG) that was to implement its ideals, activate its followers, and carry out its mandate of social reform. Nowhere in the Chicano civil rights movement has the use of the CAG been so successful as in their battles with the media, despite basic problems of disorganization, petty rivalries, lack of technical expertise, and insufficient funding. Their successes, as illustrated here and in Chapter 4, have been due to the tireless work of a few devoted activists and to the support of public interest groups and a little-known governmental agency within the U.S. Department of Justice. Together they have worked to gain access to the nation's mass media for those who, because of their cultural differences, have somehow been excluded from the mainstream of American life and who feel that the quickest road to honorable assimilation lies in communication. In the process, they have helped renew old arguments for a general right of access to the media—one that contends that the mass media consciously or unconsciously deny access to minority groups and that, by so doing, the media have created a monopoly on opinion, comment, and controversy.

One who had a great deal to do with these efforts from the beginning is Gilbert Pompa, Associate Director of the Community Relations Service (CRS), U.S. Department of Justice, who was once the assistant district attorney for the city of San Antonio. His experiences within CRS provide a historical bench mark upon which documentation of the media movement can be based.

CRS was established under Title X of the 1964 Civil Rights Act as a means of assisting minority groups in their civil rights efforts. It is designed to "help communities cope with disputes, disagreements or difficulties arising from discriminatory practices based on race, color, or national origin."[9] Since its creation, the agency has played a vital role in the civil rights movement in the areas of education, administration of justice, housing, economic development, and communications.

Gilbert Pompa explains the importance of communications in the movement, even in the beginning:

Early in the history of the Community Relations Service, when there were only three Chicanos in the agency, the three of us, on our own time, sat down for three days to draw upon our collective experience and to draft a list of what we considered the most critical areas of possible discontent affecting Chicanos nationally. Having accomplished that, we then proceeded to isolate what we considered to be the most responsive change agent that would address itself to the alleviation of that discontent, real or potential.

We spent numerous hours discussing, analyzing, and dissecting such areas as the administration of justice system, economic development, housing, health and welfare, manpower and numerous others. No matter what area we discussed or what avenue we explored, the area that continually offered the swiftest and most crosscutting vehicle for change was communications.[10]

When this was realized, CRS began to focus its attention on minorities and the mass media by sponsoring a series of media conferences. It was at these conferences that media groups organized and gained the skills necessary to challenge the communications industry on the issue of media access. But this result was more a by-product than an aim of the conferences. They were primarily set up to promote face-to-face dialogue between the media and Chicanos and between similar Chicano groups from different areas. Pompa assesses the value of the conferences this way:

... these conferences served to bring the media and local Chicanos together on an eyeball-to-eyeball basis for the first time. They accomplished two main goals which we set out to achieve. First, we sought to enable the media to hear about their deficiencies as perceived by a segment of the community whose feelings and attitudes were generally never properly ascertained or considered in the process of providing services for the community as a whole. Second, we wanted to make Mexican-Americans aware that there were alternatives within the system by which a positive change in their condition and status could be effectuated. Additionally, these conferences served, in many cases, as the basis for development of other programs conducted by CRS.[11]

THE SOUTHWEST TEXAS CONFERENCE

One of the first of these conferences was held at St. Mary's University in San Antonio, Texas, on January 18, 1969. It was the first time that Chicano activists in that city met for formal and informal discussions on media-minority problems with members of the working press. This Southwest Texas Conference on Mass Media and Mexican-Americans was sponsored by CRS, which paid for the travel expenses of many of the participants, including Los Angeles Times reporter Ruben Salazar who bluntly set the tone for the meeting in his address to the audience of media representatives and Chicano leaders:

> When [it was] suggested that I speak on the Mexican-American beat, its past and prospects, I accepted with a feeling of amused cynicism. For one thing, the Mexican-American beat in the past was nonexistent. Before the recent racial turmoil, Mexican-Americans were something that vaguely were there, but nothing which warranted comprehensive coverage—unless it concerned such, in my opinion, badly reported stories as the Pachuco race riots in Los Angeles in the early 40's, or more recently, the Bracero program's effect on Mexican-Americans.
> Therefore, there is really little to say about the Mexican-American beat in the past, except that it did not exist. Mexican-Americans traditionally kept their place so why should the big, important news media take notice of them? So that takes care of that part of the speech.[12]

The conference lasted only one day, but had important effects on the city of San Antonio in increased activity among Chicano groups interested in gaining access to the mass media. These effects will be discussed in later chapters, and it will be seen that the conference was the catalyst that was needed to begin a new era of communication and involvement for the Mexican-Americans of that city.

THE DENVER CONFERENCE

The following May 2, a conference was conducted in behalf of CRS by the Denver Metropolitan State College, under the direction of the Colorado Committee on Mass Media and the Spanish Surnamed, Inc. (CCOMMSS). The Denver-based citizen action group was formed only the week before the conference as the first formal effort of

Chicanos in Denver to deal with the mass media.[13] The conference
theme stuck to the still-popular stereotype battle: "The relationship
of mass media information and imagery to self-concept and community
status of the Spanish surnamed."[14]

Three general assumptions motivated those who planned the conference:

      1. That, in general, American mass media (radio,
TV, newspapers, magazines and books) tend to develop
conceptions of self in the Spanish surnamed of the United
States which results, in many instances, in defeated
behavior.

      2. That mass communication media in the United
States serve as part of a system that has stereotyped the
Spanish surnamed, and given these peoples a lesser status
in our society.

      3. That these mass media can instead serve to
enhance and strengthen the self-concept of the Spanish
surnamed people of the United States, with a consequent
strengthening of their performance as human beings, and
as citizens, and the raising of their status as a group in
American society.

Specific conference objectives were "to secure and develop a
delineation of the role of the mass media in developing a realistic
and positive self-concept by":

      1. Examining negative forces and patterns in mass
media communication that downgrade the self-concept and
status of these people.

      2. Identifying positive practices that now tend to
upgrade the self-concept and status.

      3. Searching for new interventions that might be
tested for their effectiveness in changing and improving
the role of the mass media vis-à-vis Spanish-surnamed
people of this country.

In this connection, the organizers sought to examine:

      1. How the mass media are a reflection of the
total system that tends to oppress these people.

      2. The extent to which mass media can be made
responsive to the needs and aspirations of these people.

      3. Ways in which these people, themselves, can
participate significantly in mass-media activities.[15]

The format for the structured discussions, which eventually led to significant minority-media agreements, was a series of six workshops conducted by experts in the fields of television, movies, newspapers, newswire services, radio programs, advertising, books, and magazines. The 250 participants and 42 media representatives were able to meet and discuss media problems with such media activists as Edward Moreno, a TV producer from Los Angeles; Carlos Conde, representing the Cabinet Committee on Opportunity for the Spanish Speaking; George Sandoval, president and general manager of radio station KAPI, Pueblo, Colorado; Nick Reyes of the National Mexican-American Anti-Defamation Committee; and John Trujillo, coordinator of Hispano studies at Metropolitan State College.[16]

Also in attendance was Palmer Hoyt, editor and publisher of the Denver Post and representatives of other media in the Denver area. Hoyt encouraged the participants at the conclusion of the all-day conference by saying that it was "high time the news media discussed the minorities and, conversely, that the minorities discussed the news media." He also told them that "the United States won't achieve its potential for greatness until groups become part of the whole show."[17] The discussion sessions were attended by other persons holding decision-making positions in the media, including John Rogers, assistant managing editor, and John Snyder, city editor (both of the Denver Post); Frank S. Hoag, Jr., editor and publisher of the Pueblo Star Journal and Chieftan; and Henry Keyes of radio station KAPI, Pueblo.[18]

Immediate recommendations from the workshops were that a dialogue be established between Chicanos and the Colorado press and broadcasting associations to promote understanding among the three groups; that Chicanos begin on the Monday after the conference to meet with the media on hiring policies and the programming needs of the community; that the media become more aware of what is happening in the Chicano community and of the background of the demonstrators; that a committee meet on the establishment of a publishing house to promote Chicano material and to improve teaching materials on Chicanos used in the schools; and that broadcasters seek federal funds for training Chicanos in journalism.[19]

But other than providing an open forum for discussion, the conference itself did little in the way of directly affecting the media. Indirectly, it served as a means of bringing people together for a common cause and allowing them to plan a course of action with the advice of experts. The plan was to begin serious dialogue with the media in the areas of employment, programming, coverage and training of Chicanos, and, hopefully to reach formal agreements. However, as the months passed following the conference, it became obvious to minority leaders that more drastic action was going to be necessary.

70

By February of the following year, nine months later, the mass-media committee and other interested Chicano groups filed petitions to deny the licenses of 45 Colorado broadcasting stations whose licenses were up for renewal. In the following months, many of the stations signed negotiated agreements rather than risk lengthy litigation and the remote possibility of losing their licenses.[20] A year later, the committee and a coalition of minority organizations entered into multimillion dollar agreements with McGraw-Hill and with Combined Communications, Inc. (to be discussed in Chapter 4).

MIDWEST CHICANO MEDIA CONFERENCE

Meanwhile, in the Midwest, Chicanos were organizing an effort by which they could gain access to the media in their region. The Midwest Chicano Committee on Mass Media was officially organized on April 18, 1970, about 10 days before the Colorado committee was formed. The action took place at Notre Dame University during a conference on civil rights attended by delegates of an eight-state area (Michigan, Missouri, Iowa, Indiana, Ohio, Wisconsin, Kansas, and Illinois). The new group immediately made plans for a media conference and outlined its goals:

1. To teach ourselves the fundamentals of the media profession.
2. To stop the stereotyping done by the advertising and media professions.
3. To open the doors for recruitment and employment within the advertising and media professions.
4. To have the Midwest schools of journalism reach out, to give the Latin communities requested advice and to recruit for potential advertising and media students.[21]

As its first official act, the new committee arranged a media conference (which was held June 20-21 at Northwestern University, Chicago) with the assistance of the Community Relations Service and the Medill School of Journalism. Conference objectives in this case were more explicit. The committee asked those planning to attend the conference to advise "other Chicano organizations in their state of the importance of this conference and to seek their active participation. . . . We cannot overly stress that those whom you invite must be specifically interested in the mass media and will hopefully act as media representatives for their organization. This conference is of special importance to publicity chairmen of the various Midwestern organizations. . . . Those attending the conference are expected to make use of all the materials provided and will be expected to organize media groups in their own communities."[22]

In this way, the Midwest conference also acted as a catalyst for media activity. Those who attended went back to their organizations armed with the knowledge of how better to use the media, and, more important, whom to contact if media problems arose.

The primary focus of the Northwestern conference was to show how Spanish-speaking citizens can exert pressure so that their communities are responsibly covered by broadcasting and print-news media. Participants were welcomed to the conference by Juan Alvarez Cuauhtemoc, president of the committee, and by Ron Dorfman, editor of the Chicago Journalism Review, who acted as keynote speaker the first day of the conference. After this, they took part in workshops dealing with radio, television, newspapers, magazines, photojournalism, and Community Antenna Television (CATV), much like those conducted in Denver the month before.[23]

But the tone of the meeting had been set before the 75 or so delegates (representing nearly half a million Mexican-Americans in the Midwest) arrived. In a preconference news release, Ramiro Borja, secretary of the committee, let it be known that this was not to be just an ordinary meeting:

> Through conferences like this, we can show the Anglo
> advertising and media professions that the cactus
> sleeper, the frito bandito, killers for Elgin watches
> and other stereotype characters they gave birth to
> better die or else . . . ![24]

As the delegates arrived, they were greeted by a challenge from within their own ranks. A communiqué from El Grito del Norte, a Chicano activist newspaper, warned them:

> No matter how friendly the Establishment press or
> individual reporters may be . . . it is basically a
> tool of the Establishment. It is dominated by Anglo
> political, economic, social and cultural power. . . .
> Only in our own press can we be sure that our side of
> the story will be presented fully and with truth.[25]

Supporters of this separatist theory argued that although it might be worthwhile to challenge the established media, in the long run, Chicanos must develop their own media.

Thus, according to Jack Williams, assistant professor at the Medill School of Journalism, "the stage was set for verbal arguments

and interruptions, which broke out repeatedly during the sessions.
. . . However, the workshops produced hours of productive advice on
how the media work and how Chicanos can use them."[26] Indeed, the
list of participants and speakers indicated that the workshops were
helpful. Besides Dorfman, other newsmen in attendance were Carol
Simpson of WBBM-AM; Ted Smart, NBC television news reporter;
Henry DeZutter, reporter for Newsweek magazine; Norris McNamara,
free-lance photo journalist; Paul Sequeira, staff photographer of the
Chicago Daily News; and Nick Rekas, president of the Chicago Better
Broadcasting Council.

Jane Redmon, a communication specialist assigned to the communications section of the Community Relations Service, helped organize the conference and was in attendance. Her description of the
atmosphere at the conference points out one of the basic problems of
the media movement: dissent from within Chicano ranks that leads
to disorganization:

> There was potential at the conference for a highly
> disruptive confrontation, but it never actually occurred.
> This was partly the result of the way the invitations
> were issued. Several prominent and knowledgeable
> Midwestern Chicanos were not invited at all, and some
> were invited only at the last minute.[27]

Among this last group, according to Miss Redmon, were representatives from Prensa Libre, a Spanish-language newspaper in Chicago known for its militancy. "They considered everyone connected
with the conference as a Tio Tomas (Uncle Tom), and were very vocal
during all the question and answer sessions." This resulted in debates
between various Chicano factions rather than between Chicanos and
Anglos. Miss Redmon felt that the Prensa Libre representatives were
"disrupting for the sake of disruption, and were challenging the 'credentials'* of the conference leaders and any participants who disagreed
with them."[28]

But despite the dissent, the conference was generally assessed
as a success and its members managed to outline solid recommendations:

---

*The "challenging of credentials" seems to be a fairly common
phenomenon within the movement. The more radical elements consider
everyone else as being "establishment" and not militant enough to be
real members of la causa.

73

1. Rely on community organization, boycott and pressure groups to acquire political force. Develop dialogue with other minority organizations. Trade experiences, secrets and techniques with them . . . form a coalition.

2. Know your numbers well. Make a thorough analysis of Chicano and Latin-American populations in your area. Use facts when you make a case for media coverage or complain of media distortion.

3. Don't feel guilty about "using" the media. Make your needs and conditions known to them. Use good public relations techniques. Send news releases to all media; make personal visits to editors, reporters, and news directors; hold news conferences; establish rapport with sympathetic editors and writers; phone-in eyewitness stories illustrating unequal treatment to Chicanos and other minorities; write letters to media officials.

4. Nonviolent demonstrations get attention from the news media. Stage marches, sit-ins. Create news through unusual actions. (Example: let Spanish-speaking students spend a day in school speaking only in their native tongue.)

5. Learn the rules and regulations of the Federal Communications Commission (FCC) regarding broadcasting. The air waves are yours.

. . . study the promises made by local broadcasters to the FCC to serve in the public interest, convenience, and necessity. Check promise against performance. When there has been misrepresentation, challenge the renewal of a station's license

. . . when the Fairness Doctrine has been violated, demand redress at once by writing to the stations and the FCC

. . . demand true community service from the specialized (ethnic) broadcasters.

6. Monitor the programing of local radio-tv stations. When distortion of the Chicano image occurs, contact the offender and press for redress.

7. If any local radio station is involved in "Call for Action" (a national project of the Urban Coalition), phone in your complaints of unequal treatment.

8. Even the best intentioned white reporters cover minority-group stories with certain preconceptions. Press the media to gain employment for your own representatives. They can become "watchdogs"

for your community. Support young Chicanos for careers in news and encourage them to be true to their heritage.

    9. Register with the Broadcast Skills Bank in your community. It is a free employment agency for minorities.

    10. Ask local broadcasters, "How many Chicanos do you have on your payroll? What kind of work are they doing?" Report inequities to the FCC.

    11. Keep cool, calm, but incessantly working to change things.[29]

NATIONAL CHICANO MEDIA CONFERENCE

A little more than a week after the Midwest conference was conducted, what could have been the most productive of all the conferences was held in the plush Savoy Room of the Plaza Hotel in New York City. Jointly sponsored by CRS and the National Urban Coalition (NUC), the meeting on June 29, 1970, was unusual in that among the participants were some of the most prominent men in the communications industry. Among the participants were Joseph H. Allen, president of McGraw-Hill, Inc.; John Gardner, chairman of NUC (now heading Common Cause); Clifton Daniel, editor of the New York Times; Katherine Graham, president of the Washington Post Co.; Randolph A. Hearst, chairman of the Executive Committee for Hearst Newspapers; Robert F. Lewine, president of the National Academy of Television Arts and Sciences; vice presidents for each of the three networks; representatives of the Ford Foundation and many others.[30]

Representing the Chicano community were the leading activists from throughout the country, including Ruben Salazar of the Los Angeles Times and the heads of many of the better-known Mexican-American civil rights organizations. Their purpose in meeting was to establish the first umbrella organization for Mexican-Americans which would oversee all media activity. The sudden surge in media-oriented activity had caused so many new groups to be formed that efforts were being duplicated and informal ties, such as with LULAC and other organizations, were not sufficient to keep everyone informed on the movement's progress.[31] The result of this conference was the formation of the short-lived National Chicano Media Council. This organization, as well as other efforts for national unity, will be dealt with in more detail later in this chapter.

THE SAN ANTONIO FCC LAW CONFERENCE

Exactly a year after the formation of the Colorado committee and the Midwest committee, a coalition of some 15 Mexican-American groups formed the Bilingual Bicultural Coalition for Mass Media (BBCMM) in San Antonio. On April 27, 1971, the organizations gathered to incorporate the committee. Its stated purpose was to assist and advise "the broadcasting industry in fulfilling their responsibilities toward the Mexican-American community by devising better methods of ascertainment and through implementation of new and effective programing."[32] The member organizations, which included the American GI Forum, the Archdiocese Commission for Mexican-American Affairs, LULAC, and others, elected Victor L. Soto as chairman and immediately set out to make up the lost time they suffered due to lack of media activity. But the San Antonio committee had the advantage of being able to learn from others' experiences, and, as a result, did not waste time deciding which direction to go. Seeing that efforts in other areas had resulted in meaningful agreements only with broadcasters, the BBCMM concentrated on the electronic media from the very beginning. The committee's first action was to conduct a conference, not on the media in general, but specifically on FCC law. Attending the session held on May 22-23, 1971 in San Antonio were five Chicano attorneys from San Antonio, two from Houston, and two from Albuquerque, as well as members of the community.[33]

It is interesting to note here the exact role that the Community Relations Service played in bringing this particular conference about, because it is typical of how the agency operates. In early May 1971, the Washington office of CRS was contacted by its Southwestern regional office in Dallas, which requested assistance in planning and conducting the conference. The regional office had been in contact with media activists through its regional communications specialist, Leo Cardenas, and the CRS field representative in San Antonio, James Perez. It was Perez who worked with the community leaders on a daily basis. After the request was approved, a Washington-based communication program assistant was assigned to help coordinate the effort. This person was Jane Redmon, who had helped with both the Denver and Chicago conferences. She was to draw up the agenda for the meeting and organize the resource materials that would be distributed. On May 12, Miss Redmon met with attorneys Jack Massie, a part-time CRS communications law specialist, and Joseph L. Gibson, a communications lawyer working with the National Mexican-American Anti-Defamation Committee (NMAADC), to outline the agenda and to draw up a list of the essential documents and materials needed. She then obtained the needed material from the FCC and duplicated the necessary number of copies. The Washington office then arranged for Bennie Williams, general manager of KALL-KQMN, Salt Lake City, to serve as the broadcasting resource at the seminar. On May 20, Miss Redmon and Mr. Cardenas flew from Washington, D.C., to San Antonio to begin last-minute preparations, along with local planners. CRS also provided travel expenses for some of the participants, as well as the outside experts who acted as seminar leaders.34

During the two-day meeting, participants learned how a broadcast station operated on a daily basis, as well as the intricacies of FCC law. Then they participated in mock negotiating sessions set up by the seminar leaders in which they took turns playing the roles of broadcaster and minority negotiator. (CRS had nothing to do with the negotiation sessions.) The problems that groups in the West and Midwest had encountered in their negotiations with broadcasters were discussed so that they would not be repeated should serious negotiations become necessary.35 An indeed, negotiations were soon to begin. Shortly after the seminar, the San Antonio committee began monitoring local stations and confronting broadcasters with demands for programming, hiring, training, and so forth. This led to a more intense negotiating workshop held on June 13, 1971, in which Coalition (BBCMM) members were rehearsed by specialists on how to conduct a negotiating session with broadcasters, and the response they could expect from the broadcasters. Below is a sample of a typical negotiating workshop:

I. The team should have a lead spokesman.
    A. Each member cannot be the main spokesman.
    B. One member should have the responsibility of guiding the negotiating team in the desired direction. He should not let the discussion be sidetracked.
    C. If the team bogs down on a point in the discussion, call a recess and straighten out the point in question among yourselves. Do not be divided. The broadcasters will be organized and well-rehearsed.
    D. If the team encounters a difficult point of law it cannot handle, move on to the next demand on the agenda until you can consult with your lawyer.
II. Ascertainment of community needs
    A. The broadcaster will inform your team that he sampled the total community and that he cannot address himself to any one segment of the community. This is a lie! FCC regulations state that minority viewpoints have to be taken into account.
    B. They will tell you that they are the experts—they will look down on you.
    C. Do not argue with them about who should represent the Mexican-American community. Just mention the names of the organizations in the coalition and state that we represent a large segment of the Mexican-American community.

D. They will tell you that you cannot tell them how they should run their station. Inform them that theirs is a public trust.
E. You can get affadavits from people who were ascertained but were not told for what purposes.

III. Petition to deny
A. Compile documentation of incidents where broadcasters have denied or refused to cover Mexican-American events or views.
B. Employment record of broadcaster should reflect the demographic breakdown of that area per FCC decision June, 1969.
C. Find instances where broadcasters have lied about ascertainment of Mexican-American persons, problems, and needs.
D. Have Mexican-Americans been able to express their views on the air? Show incidents where they have been denied.
E. Have Mexican-Americans been afforded the opportunity to develop and use local Mexican-American talent?
F. Do local Mexican-American athletes get adequate coverage and encouragement from the stations?
G. Build your brief around the 14 points set up by the FCC and how the broadcasters have applied or failed to apply these points to the Mexican-American.[36]

The results of the seminar and follow-up workshop were clear. According to Gilbert Pompa:

After the conference, the face of the city changed. It was a turning point in San Antonio from a docile, passive, seemingly content Chicano community into an active, concerned community. The Chicanos geared themselves up for an attack on the media. It wasn't completely unanimous—Senator Gonzales was outraged because he needed the media support for re-election. But the result was that the media said they would cooperate with Chicanos.[37]

The immediate outcome of the negotiations was the signing of agreements with various stations in San Antonio and the formation of a television production company by IMAGE which soon produced a one-hour television special on Mexican-Americans for national viewing. Later, the committee would enter into an extraordinary agreement with the Doubleday Broadcasting Corporation.

THE SECOND DENVER CONFERENCE

By June 24, 1972, the date of the second Denver-based media conference, the situation in the West had changed dramatically, due

78

not only to the various minor agreements negotiated after the first
conference, but primarily to the signing of the McGraw-Hill agreement,
which was the most comprehensive contract ever entered into by a
broadcaster with a minority group. Chairman Louis Trujillo alluded
to the contract in his welcoming message to the delegates:

> On May 6, 1972, an historical day for Chicanos, the
> CCMMSS, Inc., and other organizations entered into
> the largest agreement ever involving minorities; [it]
> signed [a contract] with McGraw-Hill Corporation
> involving four television stations: KLZ, Denver;
> WFBM, Indianapolis; KOGO, San Diego; and KERO,
> Bakersfield. Precedents were established for the
> beginning of a new era for Chicanos in the broadcasting
> media.

He then explained the purpose of the meeting:

> This conference is intended to provide an education in
> the various aspects of mass media and to report the
> progress being made to insure maximum utilization of
> all resources, talents, and the untapped potential of the
> Spanish-surnamed communities.[38]

Again, CRS was instrumental in planning the conference and
providing technical assistance as well as transportation for many of
the participants. In this case, coordinating assistance was provided
by Manuel Salinas, the CRS field representative for the city of Denver,
and by the author, who worked with the Washington-based communication section as a summer intern.

There were three important aspects of the conference that were
of significance to the media movement: (1) the results of a face-to-
face confrontation by the leading executives of McGraw-Hill, Inc., who
were in attendance, and Chicano activists who had recently triumphed
in the signing of the agreement; (2) the results of efforts by some of
the activists to make a second attempt to unite media groups nationally
(the National Chicano Media Council, mentioned earlier, had failed
miserably); and (3) the ability of Chicano activists to overcome petty
rivalries that threatened to damage the movement's total efforts.[39]

The first of these aspects seemed to indicate a positive trend in
minority-broadcast relationships. The local McGraw-Hill station
volunteered to film the entire conference, edit the film down to a 30-
minute documentary, air it during prime time, and turn the film over
to the committee for its own use. This the station did with enthusiasm.
The McGraw-Hill executives also seemed cordial, if not overly

enthusiastic about the recent agreement, and were willing to discuss and debate media issues with the conference participants during workshops. The second aspect can be evaluated by examining the results of an impromptu Chicano caucus held on the lawn of Loretto Heights College (the site of the meeting) while workshops were being held inside:

> At 3:00 (June 24) the leaders of the various groups gathered on the lawn. . . . Some of those in attendance were Manny Salinas (CRS), the author, Luis Trujillo (Denver), Louis Tellez (Albuquerque), Jim Perez (CRS), Frank Martinez (Albuquerque), Stephen Ximenes (Albuquerque), Victor Soto (San Antonio), and Jose Trevino (Fort Wayne, Indiana). The outcome of the meeting was an agreement by the participants that another meeting would be scheduled in the near future (possibly late July) in Washington or Denver so that all the leaders could be present to discuss a national federation of Chicano media groups.[40]

However, the meeting was never held. Instead, the continuing effort for national coordination was taken up at the Washington Radio Conference, which will be discussed below.

Perhaps the most disappointing to many Chicanos in the movement was the third aspect of importance. The Denver Conference was supposed to be national in scope, with all the important leaders from around the country in attendance. For various reasons, this never became a reality. First, because of administrative mix-ups within CRS, some of the important Chicano leaders were not provided with travel expenses they thought were coming and at the last minute found that they could not attend. But, worse, the deliberate exclusion of two nationally important Chicano media figures threatened to break up the conference. Excluded, for what appeared to be a split in the Chicano ranks, were Domingo Nick Reyes, executive director of the National Mexican-American Anti-Defamation Committee, and Dr. Daniel Valdez, publisher of La Luz, the first national Chicano magazine. Dr. Valdez, a professor at Metropolitan State College in Denver, was also one of the main organizers of the first media conference in that city. The day before the conference, Reyes met with Valdez in Denver and held a press conference criticizing the organizers for excluding them. Reyes told the media:

> The exclusion of key persons from the whole mass media campaign among Spanish speakers for visibility, ownership, and access to programing is self-destructive of the effort.

He said that the organizers

have worked into the hands of those in the country who
would prefer to keep the Spanish-speaking community
divided. The citizens' action effort among the Spanish-
speaking people is a national effort in which unity is
vitally important.[41]

The obvious attempt by Reyes and Valdez to discredit the conference publicly was one of many indications of the in-fighting that
has plagued the Chicano Movement. But, despite their efforts, the
conference seemed successful in providing a continuing education for
Chicanos in media matters and in allowing activists from various parts
of the country to gather, discuss their problems, band together, and
plan for the future.

NATIONAL SPANISH-SPEAKING RADIO SEMINAR

Next in the line of conferences was the First National Spanish-
Speaking Radio Broadcasting Seminar held in Washington, D.C., on
August 8-11, 1972. It was sponsored by Interstate Research Associates, a Chicano bilingual-bicultural consulting firm based in Washington, D.C., under a grant from the Akbar Foundation and with the
assistance of CRS. The participants reflected the whole spectrum
of Chicano life—urban, rural, Southwestern, Midwestern, male, female,
experienced, newly licensed, and those seeking broadcast licenses.
The purpose of the meeting was to allow these people to discuss their
problems face-to-face with officials of the federal agencies, representatives of the National Association of Broadcasters, and lawyers
from public interest groups. Many used their visit to the capital to
seek funding from foundations as well.[42] Upon arrival, participants
were reminded of the rationale behind the seminar:

If it is true that the pen is mightier than the sword,
then it must be said that the mass communications
industry bears an awesome responsibility to the people
it serves. If a vocal media can perpetuate racism by
projecting false stereotypes about dark skinned people,
then, it has the potential of becoming the greatest means
of peaceful social change. If an ignorant mass media is
gullible to government propaganda, then an enlightened
one can educate its audiences. However, if the mass
media become stagnant, and refuse to recognize the
prevalent social issues, then it becomes oppressive
and must be changed.[43]

81

During the course of the meeting, the delegates discussed this rationale by analyzing eight major problem areas with which Chicanos are concerned:

1. The future of radio and television (with regard to Mexican-Americans).
2. Ownership and financing of television and radio stations (a topic on which special emphasis was placed).
3. Community organization for bargaining.
4. Need for specialized technical assistance to fit the needs of the Chicano community.
5. The need for National representation in such organizations as the Federal Communications Commission and the National Association of Broadcasters.
6. The need for parity in employment and training of Chicanos on both the local and national scale.
7. The need for knowledge of the economics of a radio station.
8. The need for knowledge of the politics involved in obtaining and maintaining a bilingual radio station.[44]

After the discussions, the participants were given the opportunity to talk about their individual problems with such experts as Elbert Sampson, coordinator of public affairs for the National Association of Broadcasters; Stu Hallock, program officer for the Office of Educational Broadcasting Facilities, HEW; Joseph Zais, representative of the Broadcasting Bureau of the FCC; Albert Kramer, a communications lawyer with the Citizens Communications Center; Ralph Caprio of the Kennedy Foundation; Chester Higgins, special assistant to FCC Commissioner Benjamin Hooks; Samuel Saady, from the FCC's Department of Television; and Richard Shiben from the FCC's Department of Renewal and Transfers. Representing the Community Relations Service were Gilbert Pompa, director of national services; Jose Berrios, program assistant; and the author.[45]

To the CRS participants, who had been studying the movement for several weeks, the Radio Conference provided particularly useful insight into its problems. First, it made everyone in attendance painfully aware of the wide divergence of opinion among the activists on what the best course of action should be for Mexican-Americans with regard to the media. Those in the big cities were far ahead of their rural counterparts; they were talking of getting into CATV and challenging more broadcasters, while others had not even gained access to one radio station. Second, the participants soon came to the conclusion that little more progress could be made without a national organization to oversee and assist the multitude of Chicano media groups. (This aspect will be discussed later in this chapter.)

In order for one to understand the problem of diverse opinions, it is best to listen to the media leaders discussing their individual problems:

Stan Porras-Nebraska. "CATV sounds great, but we in Nebraska would be happy just to get one lousy radio station that serves the Chicano community with Spanish language programing. Radio is where we are at in Nebraska; CATV and TV are things of the distant future for Chicanos in our area. There are only two stations in the state that have some Spanish programing, and they are not owned by Chicanos." (Porras represents the Nebraska Mexican-American Commission which is a state department consisting of nine Chicanos and one representative from the governor's office.)

Patricio Archuleta-Colorado. "I am the new chairman of the Colorado Committee on the Mass Media and the Spanish Surnamed, a non-profit organization designed to bring change in the mass media. Although the current effort now is in implementing the McGraw-Hill agreement, the committee plans to get into CATV, distributing programing and film production. We work with the Federation of Rocky Mountain States, a loosely organized coalition of 50 organizations ranging from very conservative to very liberal. Our organization is loosely organized due to the fact that we have little financial assistance. Right now the staff consists of myself and a secretary, but in the past we have received assistance from Operation SER, CRS, The Mexican-American Legal, Defense, and Educational Fund (MALDEF), and the Citizens Communication Center (CCC)."

Bert Hernandez-El Paso. "Right now we are also in the process of implementing an agreement, but with Doubleday. We have a commitment from them to run a series of specials on Chicano culture which we are producing. Doubleday's attitude is good but we are having problems due to lack of expertise in film production. Doubleday has agreed to give us whatever we need in the way of help. Another problem we have is with the other stations in El Paso that have not signed agreements. How do you get to a station that has already had its license renewed?"

Eddie Cruz-Fremont, Ohio. "Our problem is centered around a radio station (WFRO) that has refused to air Spanish-language programing. At first the station cut down this type of programing from one hr. to one half hr. weekly and then decided to take it all off the air. The reason the station gave was that in order to comply with an FCC directive on Spanish-language programing, it had to screen all material prior to broadcasting. This meant time and money for translations

or hiring someone who could speak Spanish to monitor live programing and censor anything that might violate an FCC rule. This, he
said, was too much trouble and therefore it would be easier just to
eliminate such programing. A committee was formed to challenge
this policy and the case is now in court here in D.C. The FCC has
failed to make a ruling on the complaint for three years. The effect
is that broadcasters must take the attitude that you can't be trusted
to speak a foreign language "live" on the air. This discourages foreign-language programing and tightens the grip that a broadcaster
has on what is aired.

Tony Gomez-San Diego. "The San Diego group is involved in the implementation of the McGraw-Hill agreement. There is a Chicano Federation made up of 46 groups which has formed to battle the media. One
of the problems now is that Channel 6, the ABC affiliate, is located in
Tijuana (XETV), but does not serve the community and provides no
access. A local station, UHF-39, is trying to get the ABC affiliation
and is challenging XETV. But there is no assurance that once 39 gets
the affiliation it will serve the community any more. They refuse to
negotiate an agreement prior to a decision by the FCC. Broadcasters
along the border always use the cop-out that stations across the border
provide programing for the Mexican-American people on this side.
The truth is that they don't. There is no effort to cover community
problems." (Gomez is head of Telemetas, a project of his station,
PBS channel 15, to do research in three cities—San Diego, Tucson,
and San Antonio—as to the kind of programing needed. The project,
divided into three phases, was funded by Corp. for Public Broadcasting.) "However, now that phase I, research, has been completed, we
are told that there will be no more funds to carry out phases II and
III—pilot film and programing."
     "As for the McGraw-Hill implementation, the only problem has
been that of technical skills needed for program production now that
the commitment has been made. However, we are negotiating with
the CATV interests and we feel that the McGraw-Hill deal has given
us enough impact to negotiate with CATV."

Dante Navarro-Milwaukee. "Our problem in Milwaukee is that AM
stations have stopped their Spanish-language programing and dele-
gated it to FM stations. We tried to fight it but failed. There is a
current effort to get a Spanish FM station started in Milwaukee but it
has been unsuccessful so far. We have managed to get one station to
give us one hour five days a week. We have set up a corporation to
get our own channel and other ethnic groups have agreed to cooperate
in the enterprise, but we have no studio, equipment, or frequency."[46]

In order to obtain the power necessary to effect the many changes they feel are needed in the media, the conference delegates concluded that a national media organization was necessary. Although the media groups were in various stages of development, they agreed unanimously on a structure that would formulate a national and local strategy designed to implement numerous positions taken at the conference. The unanimous recommendations of the conference were:

1. To hold a national Chicano conference on broadcasting with major emphasis on establishing community-owned and -controlled broadcasting facilities.

2. To unify all Chicano media groups into a National Chicano Broadcasters' Association.

3. To aggresively seek the appointment of a Chicano commissioner to the Federal Communications Commission.

4. To demand the employment of bilingual, bicultural Chicanos in the media-related government agencies such as the Federal Communications Commission and the Department of Health, Education and Welfare.[47]

TOWARD A NATIONAL COALITION

By the summer of 1970, the Chicano Media Movement had spread throughout the Southwest and Midwest, and to some of the larger Eastern cities. As a result of the media conferences, literally hundreds of small, community media groups either formed or reoriented their goals to include media objectives; the knowledge they gained from the conferences was soon put to work in projects varying from the production of a tabloid newspaper to the challenging of local broadcast licenses. In fact, the movement became so widespread that few people were aware of its scope. Even within the movement itself, there was little communication between citizen action groups involved in media projects, little sharing of knowledge, and few instances of intergroup cooperation.[48] The public interest groups, such as the Office of Communication of the United Church of Christ, the Citizens Communications Center, the National Citizens Committee for Broadcasting, and Reyes's Anti-Defamation Committee, were severely taxed by the major license challenge actions and unable to give total support to all the groups seeking help. Fragmenting the movement even more was the fact that these public interest groups were in open competition for the "business" of the CAGs and uncooperative, even antagonistic, toward each other. The result was, it seemed to many observers, a rather chaotic scene, with much wasted effort and little coordination.[49] It became obvious to many of the movement's leaders that something had to be done to orchestrate the work of the many groups and to establish national guidelines and policy for Chicanos with regard to the mass media.

THE NATIONAL CHICANO MEDIA COUNCIL (NCMC)

As early as December 1969, Chicanos began to look for national coordination in their media efforts. It was then that CRS was contacted with the request that a meeting be held between Mexican-Americans and leaders of the national communications industry to bring about improvement in the performance of the industry in regard to Chicanos.[50] In March 1970, about a dozen Chicanos with strong interest in the communications field met in Washington to explore the possibility further. The meeting, financed by the National Urban Coalition, resulted in the formation of the National Chicano Media Committee which then asked NUC to sponsor a conference. It was Thomas Matthews, Communications Director of NUC, who suggested that the conference be held with the NUC Communications Task Force, made up of about 25 communications industry executives.[51]

On April 30, 1970, Nick Reyes, Armando Rendon, Bill Selden (CRS Communications Section Chief), and Tom Matthews met in Washington to formalize plans for the conference that would hopefully be the first step toward a national coalition of Chicano media activists.[52] The discussions at the meeting culminated weeks of dialogue between Chicano leaders and government and NUC officials.[53] It was agreed that a conference would take place in New York, sponsored by CRS and the Urban Coalition, to allow top media men in the country to meet with and hear the proposals of Chicano media activists. NUC agreed to defray the travel, per diem, and other costs of eight of the participants and CRS agreed to pay for the expenses of 12 others.[54] Additionally, NUC agreed to underwrite the development of a "brown paper," a comprehensive position paper on the relationship of the mass media to Chicanos, which was to be presented at the New York conference.

At the June 29 meeting in the Plaza Hotel, some of the nation's most prominent media men and women gathered to hear the presentation of the position paper and to decide on whether or not to support the formation of a National Chicano Media Council. The night before the meeting, participating Chicanos held a caucus in order to organize prior to the confrontation. In attendance were activists from across the nation: Polly Baca, Phoenix; Ruben Alfaro, Lansing, Michigan;

86

Levi Beall, Denver; Ramiro Borja, Chicago; Tony Calderon, San Antonio; Isabelle Duron, New York; Hank Lopez, New York; Ray Martel, Los Angeles; Tom Martinez, San Francisco; Eduardo Moreno, Los Angeles; Grace Olivarez, Arizona; Alberto Pena, San Antonio; Gil Pompa, Washington, D.C.; Armando Rendon, Washington, D.C.; Nick Reyes, Washington, D.C.; Raul Ruiz, Los Angeles; Ruben Salazar, Los Angeles; Frank Sanchez, Texas; George Sandoval, Pueblo, Colorado; Henry Santiestevan, Washington, D.C.; and Pete Tijerina, San Antonio.[55]

It was resolved by the group that the purpose of the presentations to the media would be to gain financial commitments from the national media people in support of a Chicano staff that would serve as a media watchdog for the Chicano Movement. Specifically, the purpose of the council would be:

> To enhance the public and private image of Chicanos in
> the United States by providing appropriate and relevant
> information, expertise and counsel to national and local
> news media, including newspapers, magazines, television
> and radio producers, motion picture producers, adver-
> tising agencies and all other media; to undertake appro-
> priate public educational efforts or other measures when
> individuals and/or public institutions persist in convey-
> ing false and degrading portrayals of any or all Chicanos;
> to undertake appropriate measures and to provide techni-
> cal assistance in support of any and all Chicanos in secur-
> ing their rights in relation to the mass media; to promote,
> develop, and/or produce news articles, audio-visual and
> other mass media presentations that will reveal the
> contributions of Chicanos to world culture generally and
> to American culture specifically.[56]

At the start of the general discussion at the conference on the 29th, the Chicanos presented a proposal for the media council that included a $65,000 annual budget for a New York office, which would supply the media with information on Chicanos and their problems and serve as a placement and recruiting center. They asked for $10,000 from each network and substantial contributions from the other media representatives.[57] By the end of the conference, Randolph Hearst, chairman of the Executive Committee of the Hearst Publications, who had recently accompanied a Chicano official of HEW on an 18-day tour of Chicano barrios, pledged $5,000. NUC also pledged its support and other media representatives gave tentative approval subject to further clarification and strengthening of the proposal.[58]

87

The proposal was based on a seven-point program centered around fighting Mexican-American stereotyping and encouraging more minority participation in the media. The New York-based organization would:

1. Generate program ideas that will assist the media in meeting the needs of the Chicano community by (a) projecting honest and realistic images of Chicanos and (b) developing programs which will educate the total society to the positive contributions of this minority community;

2. Establish a resource bank of Chicano experts in every field of Chicano endeavor who can assist the media as program consultants or information experts on the Chicano community;

3. Establish a trainee program for a skills bank of qualified Chicano writers, broadcasters, technicians, and other Chicano experts in both the electronic and print media who are qualified to be employed by media industries at all levels, including editorial boards;

4. Establish a library of information on the Chicano population at a national level for use by both the mass media and Chicano media organizations;

5. Conduct sensitivity and awareness sessions for media personnel in programming for the Chicano community;

6. Provide a vehicle for continuing communication between the Chicano community and the media personnel and policymakers;

7. Establish an on-going evaluating mechanism which will provide the media with (a) continuing information on the percentage of program time or printed space devoted to the needs of the Chicano, (b) an in-depth evaluation of programing, news coverage, and advertisements involving the Chicano community, (c) a progress report on Chicano recruitment, training and employment opportunities in the media, and, finally, (d) a periodic overview of positive performance by the media in relation to each other.[59]

After the conference, the caucus members constituted themselves as a board of directors of the Media Council and elected Ruben Salazar chairman. An executive committee of four men was also elected. Shortly thereafter the group incorporated as a non-profit organization and chose Hank Lopez (a Ford Foundation consultant) as its executive director.[60] By mid-August the new organization was in the process of producing a proposal that would be used to solicit operating funds, but it had already been provided office space by McGraw-Hill, since its president, Joseph Allen, was NUC's Communications Task Force Chairman.

But just as it seemed that the Council would be a reality, fate dealt a blow from which the organization never recovered—Ruben Salazar was killed (some thought murdered) while covering Los Angeles race riots on August 29, 1970.

THE DEATH OF A BRIDGE GAPPER

To understand the significance of the death of Ruben Salazar (sometimes called the Benito Juarez of journalism) on the media movement, one must understand the man himself. Born to a poor family in Juarez, Mexico, Salazar attended Texas Western College (now called the University of Texas at El Paso), working his way through and graduating with a B.A. degree in journalism. John Middagh, head of the Department of Journalism and friend and teacher of Salazar, remembers him as a serious, outspoken student and a "helluva good reporter."61 He soon proved his skills as a newsman, first as a reporter for the El Paso Herald Post, and later covering the Dominican crisis in 1965 on the heels of the U.S. Marines and the Vietnam war where he distinguished himself in the field of journalism. As the only Mexican-American writer for the Los Angeles Times, he became, as Hank Lopez later wrote, "our only established newspaper columnist, the most experienced and articulate Chicano writer in this whole country. Such a loss no community can afford."62 His death left the Chicano Movement in a momentary daze. Through his Times column, he had become the voice of the Civil Rights Movement and there was no one to take his place. At 42, his career was still rising, as evidenced by his appointment as chairman of the newly formed Media Council. Two months (to the day) before his death, Salazar pleaded to the distinguished members of the Communication Taskforce of NUC to "pay more attention to the despairing voices of the Chicano barrios":

> We come to you as the voice of reason and we ask you—
> almost beg you—to help us inform this nation about the
> tragic plight of eight million invisible Chicanos whose
> lives often parallel those of black people. There is much
> bitterness in our Mexican-American communities, gen-
> tlemen, and an ever increasing bitterness against school
> systems. . . . and against local and federal governments
> that apparently respond only to violence. Consequently,
> there are some Chicanos who have finally concluded that

we must have a Watts-type riot to capture your attention,
to force the establishment to pay heed.

　　We hope this won't happen. We hope that reason
will finally prevail, that you leaders of the national media
will help us push for the kinds of governmental reforms
and changes in public attitudes that will help better the
lot of the much ignored Chicano. In all candor, gentlemen,
I can't say I am entirely hopeful. It may be too late to
forestall the violence of long festering frustration, but I
think it is worth trying.63

But Salazar was not always the activist he seemed at the time
of his death. In fact, until the last year or so of his life he was scorned
by the movement as having sold out to the establishment. His career
had taken him high; as a war correspondent and foreign correspondent
for the Times in Mexico City, some felt that he had lost contact with
the barrios and with his people. Even as the Media Council was being
organized, there were those involved who thought he was too "establishment" to be invited to participate.64 It was not until he began
covering the riots of Los Angeles and the movement itself, in mid-
1969 and the summer of his own death, that Salazar became "radical-
ized." Many saw his departure from the Times in April 1970, as
evidence of his new awareness. He became news director of KMEX,
a UHF Spanish-language television station in Los Angeles, and began
producing a column for the Times on Mexican-American affairs.
According to William J. Drummond, a black reporter for the Times
and a close associate of Salazar's, "something very dramatic took
place in his writing. Opposite the editorial page he found a freedom
to express his insights and feelings that had been impossible in the
confines of reporting."65
　　A persistent topic of his column was law enforcement in the
minority community, and soon he was continually at odds with the
Los Angeles law enforcement agencies for his penchant for exploring
citizens' complaints. Drummond noticed that "his column crowded
the police more and more, bringing accusations of 'liar' from L.A.
Police Chief Edward M. Davis. There ensued a permanent estrange-
ment." But Drummond also remembers when Salazar was not the
civil rights advocate:

Ruben Salazar, as a Mexican, had paid many of the same
dues that I, a black man, had paid. We were both close
enough to our people to feel affronted by the day-to-day
indignities that they suffer, but we were trained to swal-
low emotion, because they would trim that from your
stories. You had to be low-key and factual. Ultimately,

nowhere were you secure. The Chicanos . . . distrusted
you because you were part of the Establishment, because
you weren't angry enough. And at the same time you felt
that those you worked for sometimes thought you were an
informant first and a reporter second. . . . He was a man
in the middle. . . . I knew as he did what it meant to ask
myself, "Am I part of those on top looking down, or a
part of those on the bottom looking up?" and not know the
answer.66

Perhaps it was because of his years as an objective reporter that,
even at the end, there were those who thought him too conservative.
He was forced to live a life between two worlds, one, according to
Drummond, in which he was neither a "pimp" for the revolution nor
a "shill" for the establishment.67

On that fateful Saturday of Salazar's death, the National Chicano
Moratorium Day Committee had organized the largest demonstration
ever by Mexican-Americans, assembling more than 25,000 persons
in the unincorporated county territory of East Los Angeles to protest
the disproportionately large number of Spanish-surname deaths in the
Vietnam war. Soon, violence erupted and Salazar, who had been covering the demonstration, ducked into the Silver Dollar Café to rest
and have a beer during the lull in the activity. Meanwhile, sheriff's
deputies received a report that somebody inside the bar had a gun,
although no gun was ever found. Neither Salazar nor any of the other
12 persons inside heard the warning given to evacuate the bar, according to Drummond who was manning the Times newsroom that day.
Deputy Thomas Wilson jumped across the doorway and fired a 12-inch
long tear gas grenade through a black curtain at the doorway, and the
missile struck Salazar in the skull, killing him instantly.68

After his death, only the advocate was remembered and he became
the subject of corridos (folk songs):

Adentro del Peso de Plata	Inside the Silver Dollar
Murio Ruben Salazar	Ruben Salazar died
Por la bomba de un cherif	From a sheriff's bomb
Que no se habia de usar	That should not have been used
El no murio por nada	He did not die for nothing
Murio por la libertad	He died for liberty
Murio por todos nosotros	He died for all of us
Y por nuestra unidad	And for our unity

THE DOWNFALL OF THE MEDIA COUNCIL

But instead of bringing unity, Salazar's death left the Council
without a nationally known and respected media person to lead it
through its first critical months. It is impossible to say whether the
organization would have succeeded had he lived, but certainly his
stability and moderation, as well as his respectability, were sorely
missed. Appointed as acting chairman was Tony Calderon, a television producer from San Antonio connected with IMAGE. Hank Lopez
continued to work in the capacity of executive director and tried to
organize the council's activities.[69] By April 1971, the Council was
still not funded and Lopez was concentrating on establishing personal
contact with the media to prod them into more coverage of the Chicano
movement. He was successful for a while, perhaps due to the increased
sympathy to the Chicano cause after the death of Salazar. The media
seemed anxious to follow up on story ideas mentioned by Lopez, such
as coverage on CBS "60 Minutes," a discussion of Chicano problems
on the "Merv Griffin Show," and a marked increase in coverage by
many of the nationally known newspapers and magazines.[70]

But by February 1972, Lopez was still waiting for funding.[71]
The Urban Coalition retained Lopez as a consultant for six months
and was provided office space by McGraw-Hill, but for the most part
fund-raising activities had been fruitless in obtaining a significant
amount.[72] Also, steering committee members, all of whom were
busy with their normal jobs, were scattered from one end of the country to the other, making it difficult to communicate, and, because of
a lack of money, impossible to get together often. Adding to the
Council's problems was McGraw-Hill's decision to move to a new
building in March 1972 and to withdraw its offer of free office space.
Without office or phone, the Council began communicating with executive Director Lopez at his New York residence.[73] Shortly thereafter,
Lopez either became disgusted with the whole affair or lost any hope
for the project to become funded and resigned his position in a letter
to Council members:

> Since the Media Council no longer has office space or
> telephone facilities, it seems obvious that we no longer
> have a viable status. As a matter of fact, I sense that
> most representatives of the national media probably no
> longer regard us an an existing organization since they
> are unable to contact us in New York City itself. As we
> all agreed at our initiating meeting, a national media
> office should be located in New York City which is the
> locale of the headquarters of NBC, CBS, ABC, Metro-
> media, The New York Times, Newsweek, Time, Life
> and all the other national publications. It's been my
> feeling for several months that an organization that

has no funding of any consequence will eventually be regarded as merely a paper organization. With all these factors in mind, I must frankly say that we ought to dissolve the Media Council until such time as proper funding would be available. Furthermore, since we were funded as an organization that was to "bug" the establishment, it is highly unlikely that any foundation will risk backing such an organization on pain of losing its tax-exempt status. In other words, I think it was a good effort on our part but one that seems to have faced insuperable obstacles.[74]

Thus, the Media Council never really got started, nor did it have a fair chance to prove what it could do. Nick Reyes took over the position as acting-executive director and Calderon still uses the title of chairman, but for all practical purposes the Council does not exist.

A RENEWED EFFORT

The failure of the NCMC did not remove the need for such an organization and by the summer of 1972 fresh overtures were being made to CRS to help organize a similar structure. The many victories won by CAGs due to license challenges had made the need for coordination and information even more critical. There were many who believed that the movement had been too successful in this respect—so successful that the established media suddenly lost interest in supporting a media council. Yet others, who were newer to the movement and who were unaware of the previous failure, sought national coordination. At an Albuquerque meeting on July 20, 1972, community media group representatives from California, Colorado, and New Mexico made a similar proposal to CRS.[75] Representing CRS were Willis Selden; Jane Redmon; M. O. Ortiz, Southwestern Regional Director; Julian Klugman, Western Regional Director; Carol Holgren, Southwestern Communication Specialist; and the author. The Chicano leaders were Pete Vigil (active with the San Diego McGraw-Hill agreement), Louis Trujillo of Denver, and Stephen Ximenes (chairman of the Coalition for the Enforcement of Equality in Television and Radio Utilization of Time and Hours, known as CEETRUTH, in Albuquerque). All three men were trying to implement negotiated agreements with broadcasters and were anxious to try to organize the multitude of groups that were trying to do the same thing in scattered locations throughout the Southwest. The discussion was a continuation of the one held the previous month at the Second Denver conference on the lawn of Loretto Heights College. As did the Denver discussion, this meeting also ended with a decision to get all concerned together so that the structure of the new organization could be decided upon. CRS pledged its limited support of the project and warned the activists that such an effort had already been tried and that it had met with failure.

The following month, Chicanos involved in broadcasting met for the First National Spanish-Speaking Radio Broadcasting Seminar in Washington. And once again the talk of national coordination became the major concern of the participants.[76] The conference elected an executive committee to look into the possibility of establishing a National Chicano Broadcasting Association which would act as a clearinghouse of information as well as a control center for the many separate groups. CRS in turn geared up for long-range assistance in such an effort, which it saw as a real possibility:

> Although the idea, on its face, seems to be a good one, it is not a new one. A similar effort to unify the media groups was attempted 2 years ago under the name of the National Chicano Media Council. However, there are three important differences: First, the state of Chicano media development was so embryonic at that time that all of the players were leaders without followers. The Media Council never purported to have grassroots support, and, indeed, it did not. The new organization will have the endorsement of a nationwide convention of media groups before it goes into operation. Second, the Media Council was attempted at a time when community media groups were extremely unsophisticated and unorganized. Today, many of these groups have working programs in their individual locations. Some of these revolve around sound agreements with broadcasting stations and require a tremendous amount of information and expertise to implement. Third, the Media Council attempted to set policy for all media groups rather than serve their needs.[77]

Since the radio meet in August 1972, little action has been taken to make the dream of national coordination a reality. Once again, funding will be the biggest problem, and no apparent solution has yet emerged.

NOTES

1. Frank del Olmo, "Voices for the Chicano Movement," The Quill, October 1971, p. 9.
2. Mike Esparza, "The Chicano Press," Arizona Journalist, Fall 1971, p. 6.

3. del Olmo, "Voices for the Chicano Movement," p. 9.

4. Ibid., p. 10.

5. Ibid.

6. Esparza, "The Chicano Press," p. 6.

7. del Olmo, "Voices for the Chicano Movement," p. 10.

8. Ibid., p. 11.

9. U.S. Department of Justice, Community Relations Service, Annual Report, 1971 (Washington, D.C.: U.S. Government Printing Office, 1971), p. 2.

10. Gilbert Pompa, private interview held in Washington, D.C., August 15, 1972.

11. Ibid.

12. U.S. Department of Justice, Community Relations Service, "Southwest Texas Conference on Mass Media and Mexican Americans," Washington, D.C., January 18, 1969, p. 33. Mimeographed.

13. Louis Trujillo, private interview held in Denver, Colo., June 23, 1972.

14. Colorado Committee on Mass Media and the Spanish Surnamed, "Program of the Colorado Conference on Mass Media and the Spanish Surnamed," Denver, Colo., May 2, 1970, p. 1. Mimeographed.

15. Ibid.

16. Ibid., p. 3.

17. Denver Post, May 4, 1970.

18. Denver Post, May 5, 1970.

19. Jane Redmon, interoffice memorandum concerning Colorado Media Conference, to Willis Selden, U.S. Department of Justice, Community Relations Service, Washington, D.C., May 15, 1970, pp. 1-2.

20. Willis Selden, private interview held in Washington, D.C., June 19, 1972.

21. Ramiro Borja, "Midwest Chicano Committee on Mass Media," South Bend, Ind., June 14, 1970, p. 1. Typewritten news release.

22. Ibid., p. 2.

23. Midwest Chicano Committee on Mass Media, "Proceedings of the Midwest Chicano Media Conference," Chicago, Ill., July 1970, p. 1. Mimeographed.

24. Borja, "Midwest Chicano Committee," p. 3.

25. Midwest Chicano Committee, "Proceedings of the Midwest," p. 2.

26. Ibid.

27. Jane Redmon, interoffice memorandum to Willis Selden, U.S. Department of Justice, Community Relations Service, Washington, D.C., July 8, 1970, p. 3.

28. Ibid.

29. Midwest Chicano Committee, "Proceedings of the Midwest," pp. 4-5.

30. "Agenda and List of Participants of the Chicano Media Conference," New York, N.Y., June 29, 1970, p. 1. Typewritten sheet.

31. Selden, interview, June 19, 1972.

32. James R. Perez, interoffice memorandum to Willis Selden, U.S. Department of Justice, Community Relations Service, Washington, D.C., June 16, 1971, p. 1.

33. Jane Redmon, interoffice memorandum to Willis Selden, U.S. Department of Justice, Community Relations Service, Washington, D.C., June 6, 1971, p. 1.

34. Ibid., pp. 1-2.

35. Bilingual, Bicultural Coalition for Mass Media, "Outline for Attorneys' FCC Training Workshop," San Antonio, Tex., June 8, 1971, p. 1. Mimeographed.

36. Ibid., pp. 3-4.

37. Gilbert Pompa, private interview held in Washington, D.C., July 27, 1972.

38. Colorado Committee on Mass Media and the Spanish Surnamed, "El Ano del Chicano," Denver, Colo., June 24, 1972, p. 1. Mimeographed.

39. Joe Lewels, Jr., interoffice memorandum to Charles Cogan (Acting Chief of Communications Section), U.S. Department of Justice, Community Relations Service, Washington, D.C., July 5, 1972, p. 1.

40. Ibid.

41. Denver Post, June 23, 1972.

42. Interstate Research Associates, "Summary of the First National Spanish-Speaking Radio Broadcasting Seminar," Washington, D.C., August 15, 1972, p. 1. Mimeographed.

43. Ibid., p. 4.

44. Ibid., p. 2.

45. Joe Lewels, Jr., interoffice memorandum to Charles Cogan (Acting Chief of Communications Section), U.S. Department of Justice, Community Relations Service, Washington, D.C., August 11, 1972, p. 5.

46. Ibid., pp. 1-4.

47. Interstate Research Associates, "Summary of Spanish-Speaking Seminar," p. 2.

48. Arthur Peltz (Senior Communication Specialist, Community Relations Service), private interview held in Washington, D.C., June 19, 1972.

49. Ibid.

50. Willis Selden, interoffice memorandum to Harvey Brinson (Public Information Officer), U.S. Department of Justice, Community Relations Service, Washington, D.C., June 22, 1970, p. 1.

51. Ibid.

52. Domingo Nick Reyes, letter to Thomas Matthews, May 11, 1970.

53. Selden, interview, August 28, 1972.

54. Reyes, letter to Thomas Matthews, May 11, 1970.

55. Chicano Media Committee, "Minutes of the Chicano Media Conference," New York, N.Y., June 28-29, 1970, pp. 1-2. Mimeographed.

56. Chicano Media Committee, "By-Laws of the National Chicano Media Council," New York, N.Y., August 3, 1970, p. 1. Mimeographed.

57. Selden, interview, August 28, 1972.

58. John Gardner, letter to Gilbert Pompa, July 15, 1970.

59. Chicano Media Committee, "Proposal for a Media Council to the National Urban Coalition," New York, N.Y. (undated, but probably written in August 1970), p. 1. Mimeographed.

60. Thomas Matthews, letter to Gilbert Pompa, August 10, 1970.

61. John Middagh, private interview, University of Texas, El Paso, October 7, 1972.

62. William J. Drummond, "The Death of a Man in the Middle," Esquire, April 1972, p. 77.

63. John Gardner, letter to Gilbert Pompa, September 2, 1970.

64. Selden, interview, August 28, 1972.

65. Drummond, "Death of a Man," p. 75.

66. Ibid., pp. 75-76.

67. Ibid., p. 78.

68. Ibid., p. 77.

69. Enrique Hank Lopez, letter to William Pace, April 1, 1971.

70. Ibid.

71. Joe Bernal, letter to Tony Calderon, February 10, 1972.

72. William Pace, memorandum to "Whom it may concern," February 22, 1972.

73. Enrique Hank Lopez, letter to Tony Calderon and Board Members of the National Chicano Media Council, February 29, 1972.

74. Enrique Hank Lopez, letter to the Board of Directors of the National Chicano Media Council (undated, but probably written in March 1972).

75. Joe Lewels, Jr., interoffice memorandum to Charles Cogan (Acting Chief of Communications Section), U.S. Department of Justice, Community Relations Service, Washington, D.C., July 31, 1972.

76. Interstate Research Associates, "Summary of Spanish-Speaking Seminar," August 15, 1972, p. 1.

77. Gilbert Pompa, interoffice memorandum to Benjamin Holman (Director, Community Relations Service), U.S. Department of Justice, Community Relations Service, Washington, D.C., August 17, 1972, p. 2.

CHALLENGING BROADCASTING:
RECENT HISTORY AND
PROCESS

Even in the early days of the civil rights movement, as the tactics of violence and demonstration were being refined by the blacks, it was apparent to those seeking media coverage and involvement that the media most easily influenced were those operating via the public airwaves. Lacking ownership, employment, and public-relations skills used by "establishment" organizations, minorities soon began to seek similar nonviolent alternatives for the purpose of communicating to the American mass audience. Access to the print media was seen as something less than satisfactory to civil rights leaders. Even though some newspapers supported their cause and accepted their material for publication, there was no assurance that an editor would agree to cover a particular story or even to accept a paid advertisement. No court of law in the land would force an editor to do this, as evidenced by the case of the Amalgamated Clothing Workers of Chicago who fought a fruitless battle to force the editors of Chicago papers to accept paid advertisements concerning a local labor dispute.[1] Here, one side of a controversial issue was effectively suppressed by the print media.

When Southern blacks wanted to publicize their cause, they resorted to placing an ad in the New York Times, even though few people in the South have access to that paper. The result of this action was a libel suit brought against the paper by Police Commissioner L. B. Sullivan, and the subsequent Supreme Court decision upholding the Times' printing of the advertisement.[2] But the Times' willingness to fight court battles of this type is not common among the nation's newspapers and, thus, controversial issues often do not find their way into the printed press, even in the form of paid advertisements.

Given a presidential mandate to assist minorities with their communications problems, the Community Relations Service (CRS) soon recognized the limitations inherent in dealing with the print media. As early as 1965, that agency began attempting to answer the question that civil rights leaders were starting to ask: "How do we gain access to the mass media?" The only realistic answer for solving immediate access problems was the solution offered by such public interest groups as the United Church of Christ (UCC) and the Citizens Communication Center (CCC): focus the attack on broadcasting—the point of least resistance. Thus, the course that the quest for minority access would take was charted by a few public interest lawyers, black civil rights leaders, and with the aid of an obscure government agency. All three were plagued with problems of limited resources, but made up for it with what seemed to broadcasters to be boundless energy. CRS was caught up in the broadcast movement so swiftly that it was not until 1972 that it even got around to issuing a formal policy for its professional staff members to follow with regard to the print media. When it did, the advice it offered its communication specialists throughout the United States seemed to indicate that activity in the broadcast movement had finally leveled off enough to allow the agency to devote some time to assisting minority groups in this other, almost forgotten, area. Only after substantial gains had been made in broadcasting did the movement begin to consider the print media seriously. The following is an excerpt from the CRS print media guidelines written in the summer of 1972:

> Today, even though there are bills from Congress which would force newspapers and magazines to accept advertisements, extend the fairness doctrine to the print media and establish the equivalent of the FCC for the print media, there is still no easy entry for minority groups. As a result, emphasis has been on penetrating the electronic media through the few loopholes that exist, i.e. license challenging, fairness complaints, minority agreements at a time when licenses are transferred, etc. This is not to say that there should be no effort to gain access to the print media by minorities and special interest groups who believe that they are not being fairly represented. However, the methods are different since editors are in no way obligated to print letters to the editor, news releases, editorials, advertisements, or anything for that matter.
>
> In view of these historical and dramatic differences, our programs must start with efforts to assist minorities in having an impact on the print media in the following ways: a. through employment, b. through print media ownership, c. through publicity and d. through minority advisory councils.[3]

Unfortunately for the minorities (or fortunately for the print media), CRS was not able to implement this policy. Along with the Office of Economic Opportunity and other similar agencies, CRS activities were effectively curtailed by the Nixon administration in late January 1973. The communication section was completely eliminated and the already small staff (around 300 persons in the entire agency) was reduced by two-thirds.[4]

CAGs BATTLE FOR ACCESS IN BROADCASTING

Because broadcasting is a licensed medium, and because the Federal Communications Act requires broadcasters to serve in the public "interest, convenience, and necessity," television and radio station owners are particularly vulnerable to criticism.

And public interest groups have used this vulnerability to their maximum advantage in recent years, but it wasn't always that way. Before broadcasting's vulnerability was understood, citizens would spend their time futilely trying to get their voices heard by writing letters to broadcasters, congressmen, or the FCC.

BANZHAF AND THE LAW OF EFFECTIVE REFORM

The best example of how effective criticism works is the story of the demise of cigarette smoking over the airwaves as told by FCC Commissioner Nicholas Johnson. After government reports were released telling about the dangers of smoking, hundreds of thousands of Americans wrote letters to their congressmen, broadcasters, and the FCC asking that something be done about cigarette commercials.[5]

But these letters invariably described vague feelings rather than facts. The letter writers were not specific about who had done something wrong. They did not refer to any legal principle that had been violated. And, finally, they did not seek a precise remedy. According to Johnson, many letters began, "Can't the FCC do something about . . . ?"

The answer is no! The FCC is powerless to initiate action. It must do so in behalf of the public, and the public has to know how to word its complaints in such a way that the FCC is forced into action. As a law professor at George Washington University, John Banzhaf III formed a group of law students into an organization called Action on Smoking and Health (ASH) in order to attack cigarette advertising in broadcasting.[6] The result of their efforts was a congressional ban on all cigarette advertising on both radio and television, with a resulting revenue loss to broadcasters of more than $200 million annually.[7]

Cigarette ads would probably still be on the air if it were not for Banzhaf who was able to utilize a procedure known as the "law of effective reform," outlined by Johnson in his book, How to Talk Back to Your Television Set.[8]

This basic principle consists of three parts: First, the factual basis for the grievance and the specific parties involved must be given. Second, the legal principle that indicates relief is due (constitutional provision, statute, regulation, court or agency decision) must be named. Third, the precise remedy sought (new legislation or regulations, license revocation, fines, or an order changing practices) must be stated.

Banzhaf also wrote a letter to the FCC. But he called his a "fairness complaint" under the fairness doctrine portion of the Communications Act. He specified an offender: the CBS-owned flagship station in New York City, WCBS. He said the station ran great numbers of cigarette commercials. He then referred to the legal principle known as the fairness doctrine, which provides that a broadcaster has an obligation to treat "controversial issues of public importance" fairly and to present all sides of such issues during the course of his programming.[9]

The remedy which he sought was an FCC order forcing the station to give the other side of the issue. The results of his efforts are now history. He alone did what federal officials and hundreds of thousands of concerned citizens were unable to do—forced the banning of cigarette commercials from the public airwaves.

Today, an undetermined number of citizen action groups (CAGs) from the inner-city ghettos of New York to Uvalde, Texas, are following his example with remarkable successes.

ENTER THE UNITED CHURCH OF CHRIST

Another early entry into the public access movement was the United Church of Christ's Office of Communication. Under the direction of Aaron Henry and Dr. Everett C. Parker, the office won a landmark decision when in 1966 the Court of Appeals, District of Columbia, granted the public the right to participate in the license renewal proceedings of WLBT-TV in Jackson, Mississippi.[10] This case also involved a group of students. This time they were black students from Tougaloo College in Jackson who felt that neither of the Jackson television stations, WJTV and WLBT, were representing their segment of society. With the aid of Dr. Parker, the students began monitoring the stations, and then filed a petition to deny license renewal with the FCC in 1964. The FCC denied these petitions and granted WJTV a full three-year license. WLBT was granted only a one-year license, with a warning to stop its discriminatory practices. Parker then began a long battle with the FCC. He and public interest lawyer Earle K. Moore eventually convinced the court that the Federal Communications Act requires the FCC to include the interests of the audience at renewal time. Prior to this ruling, the commission allowed only those who could prove electronic or financial injury to participate in hearings. The ruling established a precedent which has provided a legal channel through which citizen groups can voice their demands in license renewal hearings. The court also held that the renewal of the WLBT license was to be reconsidered with full, undisputed public participation.[11]

The effect of the WLBT case was to establish the public as a legal, interested party in license renewals.

Shortly after the Court of Appeals' new interpretation, a citizen action group used its new legal right successfully to prevent the transfer of a classical music radio station's license in Chicago. In Josef v FCC, the same Court of Appeals ruled in favor of the CAG and referred the FCC to Section 310 of the Communications Act that stipulates that a transfer may not be made unless a hearing is held (just as in an initial application proceeding) and that such a transfer must serve the "public interest, convenience, and necessity."[12] Following this example, two other groups protested similar transfers and in both instances the FCC was forced by the courts to allow the public to be heard.[13]

After the WLBT case, the Office of Communications began offering its services to any group requesting help. Since then, the Church has aided more than 100 groups throughout the country. It operates with funds from the Ford Foundation and instructs groups in the techniques of monitoring broadcast stations and the basics of FCC procedure.

The example set by the WLBT case was the first of many success stories, but the next major development occurred in 1969 when KTAL-TV in Texarkana, Texas, promised to hire two full-time black reporters, to make regular announcements that all area stations must consult with all substantial community groups on the area's tastes and needs, and to refrain from preempting network programs of particular interest to any substantial group without consulting with that group in advance.[14]

It was the first time that a station had agreed to share some of its sovereignty with the community. It was also the first time that citizen groups realized the extent of their powers. Station owners, afraid of losing their licenses or waging lengthy court battles, were beginning to give into demands of pressure groups.

Banzhaf's and the UCC's phenomenal successes, along with the Kerner Commission's severe criticism of the media in racial affairs, led to the formation of several more groups whose goals were to reform broadcasting. One of the most involved of these groups is the Citizens Communications Center, headed by public interest lawyer Albert Kramer, in Washington, D.C. His organization is funded by the Stern Fund, the DJB Foundation, and by the proceeds from FCC Commissioner Nicholas Johnson's book, How to Talk Back to Your Television Set.[15]

Other such groups are the Stern Community Law Firm, the Stern Concern, and the National Citizens Committee for Broadcasting (NCCB). The first of these is directed by Tracy Westen, a former aide to Nicholas Johnson. His firm operates on a $100,000 grant from the Philip M. Stern Family Fund (separate from the Stern Fund). The Stern Fund finances the Stern Concern, based in Los Angeles, which brings together the research and informational resources available in Washington with the creative talents in Los Angeles, in an effort to "hasten the pace of social change."[16] The National Citizens Committee for Broadcasting operates in conjunction with the Media Committee of the United Presbyterian Church. Jane Goodman, the committee's administrative director, also works as Dr. Everett Parker's aid in the affairs of the UCC's Office of Communication as its director of field programs. Currently, she is concentrating her efforts on finding ways to fund the groups that have already negotiated agreements with broadcasters, but which are in trouble because of lack of financing.[17]

By early 1970, the lessons learned in previous cases had a chance to be refined in a massive effort to make the broadcast stations of Atlanta, Georgia, more responsive to the community needs of blacks.

Local blacks joined forces and called on both the Office of Communications and the Citizens Communications Center for assistance. The goal of challenging all 28 local outlets required a massive effort. Blacks were divided into negotiating teams, and local attorneys were recruited and briefed by Kramer. Mock negotiations were held to prepare the teams to deal with station managers. (CRS has been involved in the detailed planning of such meetings since the WLBT case.)

Eventually, statements of policy acceptable to both sides were obtained from 24 stations, and petitions to deny license renewals were filed against four. Two of these suits were later withdrawn when the stations decided to give in.[18]

Today, the techniques that were developed and refined in Atlanta are being used from one end of the country to the other with astonishing success and there seems to be no end to the trend.

It is little wonder that the National Association of Broadcasters (NAB) sees the trend as an organized movement and as a major threat to their broadcast freedom of the press. But, so far, cries by broadcasters of First Amendment violations have gone unheeded. The courts have almost invariably sided with citizen groups, even when it meant reversing FCC decisions that favored broadcasters.[19]

FCC POLICY STATEMENT CHALLENGED

The CCC, along with Black Efforts for Soul in Television (BEST), fought and won yet another battle for increased public access to the media. Both groups joined forces in June 1970 and filed a petition for rule making with the FCC.[20] The effort was made in order to prevent the commission from changing its 1965 "Policy Statement on Comparative Hearings" which was favorable to public interest groups.[21]

This policy established guidelines for license renewal hearings which specified that licenses could only be renewed on a comparison basis. The areas of comparison and evaluation were diversification of control of the media of mass communications, full-time participation in station operation by owners, proposed program service, past broadcast record, and efficient use of the frequency. Although this was the FCC's policy, the two groups filing the petition felt that a rule would serve to clarify and substantiate the hearing procedure in favor of the public. Thus, the rule proposed by the groups was similar to the 1965 policy. However, the very day that the petition was being considered, the FCC adopted a revised policy called the "1970 Policy Statement on Comparative Hearings Involving Renewal Applicants," which altered the original policy considerably in favor of the broadcaster.[22] The policy was similar to the commission's remarks before Senator John Pastore's (D-R.I.) Subcommittee on Communications, on Senate Bill 2004. The bill and the policy would deny competing applicants a complete hearing unless the service of the incumbent licensee could be found lacking. Commissioner Nicholas Johnson, the only one to voice a dissent over the policy, said:

> The country has long believed that the public will be better served over the long run by free and open competition. Now, not only can the industry win every ball game; it is in a position to change the rules.[23]

The groups eventually appealed to the Court of Appeals in the District of Columbia to intercede. The court ruled that the 1970 statement would, in effect, prevent the new applicant from competing effectively for a broadcast license:

> Thus, without impinging at all upon the commission's substantive discretion in weighing factors and granting license, our holding today merely requires the commission

to adhere to the comparative hearing procedure which it has followed without fail since Ashbacker [24] and which has rightly come to be accepted by observers as a part of the due process owed to all mutually exclusive applications.[25]

The effect of this ruling was to nullify the 1970 policy statement. The FCC has asked for comments from all concerned about the problem, but, meanwhile, further legislation on the subject has been introduced in Congress which would give the competitive advantage to the broadcaster.[26]

In late 1972, broadcasters and the National Association of Broadcasters geared up for the political drive to gain congressional relief in the area of license renewals. The NAB's task force on license renewals met in the last week of November 1972 to plan an intensive campaign to reduce effectively the public's right to intervene or compete during license renewal hearings for a broadcast station.[27] Senior House Commerce Committee members assured the NAB that there would be hearings on the problem perhaps as soon as March 1973. Toward this time, the NAB also revitalized its legislative liaison committee, which consists of "captains" in each of the 50 states, with each congressman assigned to one or two broadcasters who live in his district and who have good relations with him. Also included in the lobbying effort are the state broadcaster associations, a national public relations campaign, and a program to enlist support of community leaders for the broadcaster's viewpoint.[28]

But even as these efforts were being organized, congressmen were lining up in long queues to give the broadcasters the protection they sought. More than 130 separate renewal bills were introduced in both houses during the 92nd Congress, most of which were based on a measure offered in December 1971 by Congressman James T. Broyhill (R-N.C.) and based on draft legislation prepared by the NAB.[29] It provides five-year license periods (instead of the three-year periods now in effect) for broadcasters, thereby reducing the frequency with which their licenses can be challenged. It also stipulates that, in a hearing, the incumbent licensee would be granted renewal if during the preceding license period he had shown "a good-faith effort" to serve the community and had not demonstrated "a callous disregard for law or the (FCC's) regulations." Needless to say, there are many variations of this bill, but all of them protect the broadcaster at the expense of the competing applicant. Some of the bills would extend the renewal period to five years but not alter the renewal process, while others would do just the opposite.

As of mid-1972, broadcasters had contacted 528 members of Congress and had received pledges of support from 256 representatives and 49 senators. Only three congressmen and two senators had spoken in opposition, and 89 Democrats and 86 Republicans sponsored one or more of the 130 or so bills. The NAB has also established a political-action committee to raise funds and make contributions to candidates in an effort to gain help in Congress.[30]

Opposition to the bills will come from the UCC, CCC, BEST, and other public-interest groups.

One of the most publicized proposed bills was that of the White House Office of Telecommunications Policy, which would provide for a five-year license period and require the commission to find that an incumbent's record did not merit renewal before it could call a hearing to consider new applications. It would also bar the commission from setting quantitative standards for judging renewal applicants.[31] In effect, it would grant the broadcasters the protection they seek.

Thus, the scene is set for what appears now to be an inevitable landslide victory for broadcasters, and ultimately the end of public participation and competition in the field of electronic broadcasting. However, much has already been accomplished by public-interest groups in the areas of programming, minority hiring and training, minority advisory councils, and in many other areas. Now that it can be understood more clearly, it is well to outline the specific efforts of the Chicano Movement in media access with regard to broadcasting.

NOTES

1. Chicago Joint Board, Amalgamated Clothing Workers v. Chicago Tribune Co., 307 F. Suppl. 422 (1970).

2. New York Times Co. v. Sullivan, 376 U.S. 245 (1964).

3. U.S. Department of Justice, Community Relations Service, "Guidelines for Community Relations Service Programing with Respect to the Print Media," Washington, D.C., August 30, 1972, p. 1. Mimeographed.

4. Willis Selden, telephone interview, February 5, 1973.

5. Nicholas Johnson, "The Easy Chair," Harper's, February 1969, p. 44.

6. Banzhaf v. The Federal Communications Commission, 405 F. 2d 1082 C.A.D.C. (1968).

7. Joe Lewels, Jr., "Expansion of the Fairness Doctrine," Freedom of Information Center Report No. 251, November 1970, p. 1.

8. Nicholas Johnson, How to Talk Back to Your Television Set (Boston: Little, Brown & Co., 1969), p. 202.

9. 405 F. 2d 1082 C.A.D.C. (1968).

10. Office of Communications, United Church of Christ v. The Federal Communications Commission, 359 F. 2d 997. (1966).

11. 359 F. 2d 944, 1006 (1966).

12. Josef v. The Federal Communications Commission, 404 F. 2d 207 (1968).

13. Citizens Committee v. The Federal Communications Commission, 18 RR 2d 2021 (1970).

14. David C. Loveland, "Citizen Groups Challenge Radio-TV," Freedom of Information Center Report No. 256, February 1971, p. 3.

15. Leonard Zeidenberg, "The Struggle over Broadcast Access," Broadcasting, September 20, 1971, p. 37.

16. Ibid.

17. Jane Goodman, private interview held in Washington, D.C., August 15, 1972.

18. Zeidenberg, "The Struggle over Broadcast Access," p. 36.

19. Loveland, "Citizen Groups Challenge Radio-TV," p. 1.

20. 21 FCC 2d 355 (1970).

21. 1 FCC 2d 393 (1965).

22. FCC 70-620, 18 RR 2d (1901).

23. 18 RR 2d (1902).

24. Ashbacker v. The Federal Communications Commission, 326 (U.S.) 327, 330 (1945).

25. 22 RR 2d 2001, 2017.

26. "Senate Bill Appears for Renewal Protection," Broadcasting, October 4, 1971, p. 6.

27. "NAB Presses Drive for Renewal Relief," Broadcasting, December 4, 1972, p. 38.

28. Ibid.

29. "Whitehead Bill Joins the Crowd Seeking to Ease Renewal Trauma," Broadcasting, January 1, 1972, p. 24.

30. Ibid., p. 25.

31. "The Dust Hasn't Settled after Speech by Whitehead," Broadcasting, January 1, 1973, p. 18.

5

CHICANOS CHALLENGE
BROADCASTING

Armed with the knowledge provided them by the public-interest law groups, Chicanos began looking toward the electronic media in the late 1960s as a primary objective in their civil rights movement. The lessons learned and the legal victories won by Banzhaf, the United Church of Christ (UCC), the Citizens Communications Center (CCC), and the black groups were soon put to use in the Southwest. The particular areas of vulnerability for broadcasters—the license renewal, the license transfer, and the initial license application—were seized upon by a multitude of ad hoc organizations with the tenacity of a Gila monster. Like the Southwestern reptile, once they had a hold on their victim, there was no letting go until the victory was won.

It is well to note here the nature of these citizen action groups with respect to their organization and coordination. From the outside it might appear that the Chicano Movement in the media was well orchestrated in that dozens of groups at the local level became involved in license challenges at the same time. This would seem to indicate an infrastructure such as that of an organization like the Anti-Defamation League of B'nai B'rith in which national and regional offices dictate policy and pass information to their local chapters. Such is not the case with the Chicano Movement. For example, the Colorado Committee on Mass Media and the Spanish Surnamed in Denver is not connected in any way (except perhaps philosophically) with the Bilingual Bicultural Coalition on Mass Media in San Antonio. During the legal battles they pursued independently of each other, the Colorado group worked with the CCC, while the San Antonio group worked with the UCC and the National Mexican-American Anti-Defamation Committee (NMAADC). Although the NMAADC, under the direction of Domingo Nick Reyes, was established for the purpose of representing Mexican-Americans in media affairs, it was never able to gain the support of many of the media groups at the local level that were formed independently. This was due mainly to rivalries and in-fighting within the movement that have plagued all efforts to achieve national coordination. Therefore, there is virtually no national or regional linkup between the many groups, except that provided by the Community Relations Service (CRS), which is the only organization that is in constant contact with all of the groups, as well as with the public-interest law groups. Through a network of field representatives, stationed in every major city in the U.S., and through financial support at times of conferences, CRS has served as an informal communications network for minorities ever since the first license challenge in Jackson, Mississippi. The primary difference between the Chicano efforts and organizations such as the Anti-Defamation League of B'nai B'rith is that the former grew from the bottom up. That is, the organizers came from the lower strata of society, as part of a social movement, rather than being organized by a central committee.

THE CHALLENGE GAME BEGINS

One of the first indications that Chicanos were becoming involved in the challenge game came on October 6, 1970, when a San Antonio-based group called Involvement of Mexican-Americans in Gainful Endeavors (IMAGE) and the Mexican-American Legal, Defense, and Educational Fund (MALDEF) joined forces to petition the FCC to deny the license of KVOU-AM in Uvalde, Texas.[1] Grievances listed included claims that overall programming was irrelevant and nonresponsive to the social, economic, and educational needs of Mexican-Americans and that the station failed to provide employment opportunities to Mexican-Americans. Ultimately, the station's license was renewed by the FCC, but the action did not seem to dampen the enthusiasm of the challengers. By the following March, as Colorado stations were preparing for their license-renewal deadline, citizen groups were ready and waiting. The first stations to be hit with denial petitions were KLZ-TV and KOA-AM, both in Denver. This action was soon followed by similar petitions against some 45 Colorado radio and TV stations, mostly in the Denver area.[2]

A half dozen citizen groups—including committees of black and Spanish-surnamed Americans—participated in the petition to deny the renewal of KLZ-TV, owned by Time-Life Broadcast, Inc. KOA's renewal application was the target of two groups—the Committee of Concerned Citizens for a Responsible KOA and the Colorado Citizens Committee for Broadcasting. Both were also among the groups seeking denial of KLZ's license. The group filing against the 45 stations was the Colorado Committee on the Mass Media and the Spanish Surnamed (CCOMMSS), one of the groups involved in the KLZ petition.

Already the protesting groups' complaints began to bear some similarities that were to be seen time and again as the movement grew. Three basic complaints were the most common: first, the groups claimed that broadcasters do not check the minority groups well enough in ascertaining community needs. (The FCC requires broadcasters to survey the community needs as part of the application requirements.) Second, they claimed that stations do not carry programs that serve the needs of the minority group. Third, the groups complained that stations discriminate against minority groups in their hiring practices.[3]

These and other complaints were part of the reason that the Bilingual, Bicultural Coalition for Mass Media (BBCMM) filed petitions against WOAI-TV, KSAT-TV, and KITE-AM in the summer of 1971.[4] The coalition had already reached formal agreements with KENS-TV and some radio stations.[5] It was not until November 1972 that the FCC got around to making a ruling on the KSAT renewal in favor of the broadcaster.[6] The commission said that the station had complied with the requirements in ascertaining the needs of the community and that the station made a good faith effort to meet its programming obligations. The same month, the FCC approved the renewal of WOAI-TV in a 5-2 decision, with commissioners Benjamin Hooks and Nicholas Johnson dissenting, as in the KSAT case.[7] Both decisions came at a time when the FCC was inundated with more than 100 petitions to deny. The final challenge, to KITE-AM, was successful when the Doubleday Broadcasting Company entered into an agreement with the coalition that included three of its other stations in the Southwest. The details of this and other significant agreements will be discussed in a following section.

Simultaneous to the San Antonio petitions was a victory by the Dallas-Fort Worth Coalition for the Free Flow of Information (CFFI), which gained concessions from five stations on employment and programming practices.[8] The CFFI, composed of 17 groups of blacks, whites, Mexican-Americans, and American Indians, reached agreements with WBAP-TV, KBUY-FM, WFAA-TV, KXOL-AM, and KDFW-TV. The coalition never filed a petition to deny, but threatened to do so if an agreement was not reached.

Meanwhile, in New Mexico, the Alianza Federal de Pueblos Libres, representing 3,000 families of Mexican descent, fought a slightly different battle in Albuquerque.[9] Its major effort in 1971 was the initiation of action against KOB-TV, KOAT-TV, and KGGM-TV to obtain financial records. The Stern Community Law Firm, Citizens Communication Center, and the National Citizens Committee for Broadcasting joined the Alianza in petitioning for disclosure. Their argument was that the adequacy of the station's programs must be judged, in substantial part, by the extent to which it reinvests an adequate percentage of its profits in locally-originated and community-oriented programming.[10]

The Federal Communications Commission saw it differently. In a 6-0 decision the commissioners said it was not in the power of the FCC to authorize disclosure on the chance that it might help a petitioner. The petitioner must first show that disclosure is a necessary link in the chain of evidence to resolve a public issue. Yet, even if the Alianza had demonstrated the relevance of the disclosure to their case to the satisfaction of the FCC, the annual financial reports as presently constructed are not designed to provide information on specific expenditures for such categories as news, public affairs, and local programming. To allow disclosure would mean departure from the historical confidentiality of this type of information. Such a departure would have to come through a general rule-making proceeding.[11]

Defeated in their attempt to get the records, the Alianza filed a petition to deny the licenses anyway. The specific failures were noted: few if any programs included the land grants issue; the ETV station served as a forum for propaganda of the Albuquerque Public School System; the lack of responsible programming for the Mexican-American community created the conditions that led to the civil disturbances of June 13-16, 1971, when the rioting was directed against the police, the seat of the city government, the business community, and especially the media.[12]

The Alianza lost the second round, but the next petition filed—against KDEF-TV in Albuquerque—brought concrete results. This station, as a part of the Doubleday Broadcasting Company system, negotiated demands in conjunction with three other Doubleday stations in Texas. The Doubleday capitulation came after its Odessa, Texas, station, KOSA-TV, and its El Paso station, KROD-TV, had citizen group petitions filed against them.[13] Local petitioners in these cases had the assistance of the National Mexican-American Anti-Defamation Committee, Inc., which had also been working to prevent the sale of five television stations by Time-Life Broadcasting to McGraw-Hill.

At the same time, the United Church of Christ was aiding another group in Albuquerque in their independent petition to deny the licenses of KDEF-AM (Doubleday) and KGGM-TV. The Alianza had already filed against KGGM. There is no connection between the various groups, other than common goals. The new group was the Coalition for the Enforcement of Equality in Television and Radio Utilization of Time and Hours (CEETRUTH), which represents 19 Chicano organizations.[14] The coalition charged that KGGM-TV employed too few members of minority groups and that the University of New Mexico station failed to ascertain the community needs satisfactorily.[15]

Challenge fever also was running high in California, where a virtual gold rush for broadcast licenses took place as the November 1,

1971, deadline for formally notifying the FCC of a petition action drew nearer. In San Francisco, the Community Coalition for Media Change, which included Chicano groups, negotiated with five bay area stations asking that they program in a way that reflects "the distinctive desires, tastes, needs, interests, and cultures" of the various ethnic groups of the area.[16] In San Jose, the Committee for Open Media filed petitions against KRON-TV and KPIX-TV and accused them of violating the First Amendment by failing to provide an adequate forum for the discussion of public issues.[17] Other stations hit with petitions to deny were ABC's KGO-TV, NBC's KNBR-AM-FM, RKO General's KFRC-AM and KFMS-FM, all in San Francisco. By the time of the deadline for petition, 18 had been filed against the renewal applications of 17 stations, including nine television outlets and two AM-FM combinations. Other affected by the petitions were KTVU-TV, Oakland (challenged by the California La Raza Media Coalition, along with 17 other Spanish-surnamed groups), KEST-AM and KOFY-AM both in San Francisco.[18] Elsewhere in the state, petitions were filed against KJTV-TV and KWAC-AM, both Bakersfield, by, respectively, Kern Council for Civic Unity and by the Community Service Organization and the United Farm Workers Organizing Committee, headed by Cesar Chavez. KOGO-TV in San Diego was challenged by the Chicano Federation of San Diego County and KCOP-TV and KGFJ-AM, both in Los Angeles, were challenged by the Council on Radio and Television. Both the UCC and CCC were active in aiding the various groups,[19] while CRS provided information and liaison between the groups and other agencies.

Chicanos elsewhere in the country were also in the act. In Oregon, the Valley Migrant League, under the leadership of Joaquin Montemayor, began negotiations with KPTY-TV, Portland, and KVDO-TV, Salem, in July 1971. Chicanos there had formed a group called the Northwest Chicano Mass Media Systems.[20] Chicanos in Washington, D.C., under the direction of the NMAADC, organized a drive to challenge the licenses of all the city's radio and television stations in April 1972.[21] Rodolfo (Corky) Gonzales' Crusade for Justice joined the Colorado Committee in its petition against KWGN-TV in Denver and against KPUB-TV in Pueblo, as well as filing its own petitions to deny against KABC-TV and KNBC-TV in Los Angeles.

This shotgun approach, as it was termed by broadcasters, was not entirely effective in gaining concessions from the electronic media. Many of the licenses have been renewed by the FCC in spite of the petitions to deny. Examples of these are KIIX-AM-FM, Fort Collins, Colorado,[22] and KWGN-TV, Denver,[23] both of which were being challenged by the Colorado Committee on Mass Media and the Spanish Surnamed. The latter FCC decision is being appealed to the Court of Appeals, District of Columbia.

Still, many stations, rather than become involved in lengthy litigation, succumbed to the pressures and signed formal agreements to provide more access to Chicanos. Typical of these are those of KQEO-AM in Albuquerque with CEETRUTH, which provides for six steps affecting changes in program and employment practices at the station.24 KEST-AM in San Francisco signed an agreement with the Joint Action and Strategy Committee and the Northern California Council of Churches calling for expanded minority programming and a $15,000 settlement by the station with a group of former employees.25 In early 1971, Chicanos in Fresno benefited from an agreement negotiated with Capital Cities Broadcasting Co. affecting the three cities in which it sought to purchase broadcast properties (New Haven, Connecticut, and Philadelphia were the other two cities). Minorities in those cities were assured a voice in the production of $1 million of local programming over a three-year period.26

But without doubt the most far-reaching agreements were those entered into by KABL-AM-FM, Oakland-San Francisco, and by four stations owned by McGraw-Hill. The first was unique in that it came at the request of the owners, without a petition's ever being filed. The Starr brothers of New Orleans and William F. Buckley, Jr., approached La Raza Media Coalition and the Community Coalition for Media Change to do something for the community when they purchased KABL.27 The result was a precedent-setting agreement whereby minority people sit on the board of directors of a multimillion dollar corporation and are given stock ownership. The contract calls for investment by the station of $50,000 in minority training programs, promotion of minorities to top-level management within the three-year license renewal period of the station, an affirmative hiring program, including community liaison personnel, and programs dealing with community problems.

The McGraw-Hill Agreement, which includes KLZ-TV, Denver; KOGO-TV, San Diego; KERO-TV, Bakersfield; and WFBM-TV, Indianapolis, was the result of a challenge to McGraw-Hill's attempt to purchase these and one other station from Time-Life, Inc. The Citizens Communication Center and the NMAADC were instrumental in organizing a five-city coalition of eight Mexican-American groups and one black group in one massive effort.28 The terms of the agreement provide that McGraw-Hill not purchase one of the stations it proposed to buy (WOOD-TV, Grand Rapids). This part of the agreement, engineered by Albert Kramer of CCC, was designed to enforce the FCC's top 50 market policy. The policy is supposed to promote diversification of ownership in those markets by prohibiting a broadcaster from acquiring more than two VHF stations in the top 50 markets without showing "a compelling public interest." (By FCC standards, markets are ranked according to the largest net weekly circulation of any station in each, as reported by the American Research Bureau.) Kramer called this portion of the agreement the most significant because it is the first enforcement of the top 50 market policy since its adoption in 1968. He calls it "the private enforcement of a public law."[29] (The second portion of the agreement is detailed in the following section along with other significant agreements involving Chicanos.) The Mexican-American groups that opposed the station sales are the Colorado Committee on Mass Media and the Spanish Surnamed, the Chicano Federation of San Diego County, the Community Service Organization of Bakersfield and Los Angeles, the Associated Migrant Opportunity Services of Indianapolis, and the Latino American Council, Sociedad Mutualista Circulo Mexicano, and Club Latino Jalisco, all of Grand Rapids. Besides CCC and UCC, they were represented by the Mexican-American Legal Defense and Education Fund.[30]

ANALYSIS OF BROADCAST AGREEMENTS

The following is a systematic breakdown of a sample of the various broadcast-Chicano-group agreements that have been negotiated. The agreements are broken down into their basic elements, and the terms of each contract in each of nine major areas are summarized. Table 1 illustrates at a quick glance the common elements of the various agreements and the city and station to which they apply.*

Advisory Councils

A. McGraw-Hill Agreement (KERO-TV in Bakersfield, California, KOGO-TV in San Diego, KLZ-TV in Denver and WFBM-TV in Indianapolis):

    Minority Advisory Council (MAC). Membership of this five-member council will be divided between Chicanos and blacks. Each of the four cities in which McGraw-Hill acquired stations will have a council to act as consultants to station management in the planning and production of programs in the interest of minorities and in recruitment and training of minorities for station employment.

    National Minority Advisory Council. Two delegates (one Chicano and one black) from each MAC will meet annually with the

---

*Information used in this analysis was obtained from the station files at the Federal Communication Commission, Washington, D.C. Copies of agreements may be obtained at the FCC document library by asking for station file by call letters.

TABLE 1

Common Elements of Current Broadcast-Chicano Agreements

Station	City	Training	Advisory Council	Ascertainment Program	Employment Program	Programming	Sensitivity Training	Minority Business Aid	Scholarships	Public Service Announcements
McGraw-Hill										
KLZ-TV	Denver	x	x	x	x	x		x		x
KOGO-TV	San Diego	x	x	x	x	x		x		x
KERO-TV	Bakersfield	x	x	x	x	x		x		x
Doubleday										
KDEF-TV	Albuquerque	x	x	x	x	x	x	x	x	
KITE-TV	San Antonio	x	x	x	x	x	x	x	x	
KROD-TV	El Paso	x	x	x	x	x	x	x	x	
KOSA-TV	Odessa	x	x	x	x	x	x	x	x	
Combined Communications										
KBTV-TV	Denver	x	x		x	x	x			
KARK-TV	Little Rock	x	x		x	x				
KOA-TV-AM-FM	Denver	x	x	x	x	x		x	x	
KQEO-AM	Albuquerque	x	x		x	x				x
KTRK-TV	Houston		x		x	x	x			x
KXOL-AM	Ft. Worth		x		x	x			x	x
KBUY-FM	Ft. Worth	x	x	x	x	x			x	x

115

president of the McGraw-Hill broadcasting group to coordinate the local MACs and serve as an appeal board for the local groups.

Minority Affairs Coordinator. A Chicano and a black will serve alternating one-year terms as national coordinator.

B. Doubleday (The Doubleday Broadcasting Company stations involved are KITE in San Antonio, KROD in El Paso, KOSA in Odessa, and KDEF in Albuquerque):

Chicano Local Advisory Committee. Seven members will meet monthly with the manager of the local station to advise on ascertainment of community needs and service, employment, training, scholarships, programming, economic development, and any other matters relevant to Chicano communities.

Corporate Advisory Committee. A representative from each station will select a fifth member at large and a NMAADC representative will serve in ex-officio capacity. The committee will meet semiannually with Doubleday to advise in the areas detailed above with observers from the United Church of Christ or other such persons attending at will.

C. Combined Communications (KBTV-TV in Denver and KARK-TV in Little Rock are the two stations affected):

KBTV (Denver). A Minority Advisory Council will be chosen by the Denver Task Force for Community Broadcasting to help the Combined Communications Corporation (CCC) carry out its agreements in regard to minority employment and programming. CCC will appoint a full-time station staff member with the primary task of assuring effective coordination with the Task Force.

KARK-TV (Little Rock). Representatives of the Ad Hoc Coalition on Broadcasting will be designated by the coalition as an advisory council. The six-member committee would meet monthly to advise on ascertainment of community needs, recruitment, training, programming, etc.

D. KTRK-AM-FM (Houston):

Advisory Panel. A black and Chicano panel will advise KTRK regarding the needs and interests of the community and will meet periodically during the year for program suggestions.

E. KQEO-AM (Albuquerque):

The station will consult regularly with an advisory group suggested by CEETRUTH on news presentations, community problems, and coalition viewpoints. This group will serve as a channel for grass roots minority opinion to reach station news, programming, and management personnel.

F. <u>KOA-TV-AM-FM</u> (Denver):
   Although not set up as an advisory council per se, the Colorado Committee will counsel the station on minority programming.

G. <u>KBUY-FM</u> (Fort Worth):
   KBUY will meet on a quarterly basis with a committee desig-- nated by the Greater Fort Worth Coalition for the Free Flow of Information.

H. <u>KXOL-AM</u> (Fort Worth):
   A committee selected by the Greater Fort Worth Coalition for a Free Flow of Information will meet quarterly with the station manager.

Ascertaining Community Needs

A. <u>McGraw-Hill</u>:
   An ongoing ascertainment program will be set up under the supervision of the MAC, the station public affairs officers, and the station employees.

B. <u>Doubleday</u>:
   Ascertainment of community needs will be made under the guidance of the Local Advisory Committee and employment parity attempted. FCC guidelines are to be followed in the areas of activities, program, interests, needs, tastes, culture and positive aspects of the Chicano community.

C. <u>KQEO-AM</u> (Albuquerque):
   Access will be provided for minority groups to present editorial opinions; meetings will be arranged between station news and programming staff and minority groups so that the station staff may, through direct dialogue, learn about minority group views.

D. <u>KBUY-FM</u> (Fort Worth):
   KBUY-FM will regularly announce on the air that the station will consult with all substantial groups in the community regarding the tastes and needs of that community and will accept suggestions on how best to render service that will accommodate those tastes and meet those needs. This

announcement will be broadcast once a week, on a weekday, between 8 a.m. and 7 p.m.

Employment

A. McGraw-Hill:

Employment. At least 15 percent of the employees at the four stations must within three years be from minority groups, at least 10 percent of each outlet. The goal is to have a distribution between Chicanos and blacks approximating their demographic relationship in the composition of the area, also between males and females approximating their work proportion within the work force. Of minority employees at each station, at least 25 percent must be in professional, managerial, and sales as well as technical categories, by the end of the first year of McGraw-Hill management. A management-level minority employee shall serve as a member of a three-member editorial board at each station. Training programs will be established from which to draw. Three minority persons are to be trained in each of the three larger markets and two in Bakersfield.

B. Doubleday:

Parity in employment will be attempted through advisement from the Local Advisory Committee and the Corporate Advisory Committee. Within six months of the filing of the agreement (March 1972) local stations will employ one Chicano news reporter. KROD will utilize a Chicano newsman as an anchorman on a daily news program, as will KOSA, whenever it creates another news program; if none, KOSA will utilize a Chicano newsman on a regular biweekly basis as a host to an issue-oriented program. One station employee will serve as liaison and community-relations representative to the Chicano community.

C. Combined Communications:

KBTV (Denver). CCC will try to obtain a ratio of black and Chicano employment of 9.1 percent and 14.6 percent respectively. This effort will include appropriate training of qualifiable minority applicants. KBTV will immediately see that two minority member newsmen appear on camera on a regular basis and within one year CCC will employ additional reporters (one black, one Chicano) who will be trained to qualify them for regular on-camera appearances. Efforts will be

118

made to permit minority members to qualify for management
positions.

KARK-TV (Little Rock). Combined Communications Corporation
will actively seek minority employment proportionate to the
number of minority persons in the metropolitan area. Employment will be open in all areas. Within one year, KARK will
employ three full-time blacks in its news department. Of
these three, one will be a male news reporter who will appear
on camera.

D. KTRK-AM-FM (Houston):

The station will broadcast "Job Bank" twice a week plus prime-
time specials directed to minority problems in employment.
No specific station commitments were made in relation to
hiring minorities; however, the station already employs some.

E. KQEO-AM (Albuquerque):

A Chicano will be hired for the news staff to cover in-depth
barrio news so that Chicano viewpoints may be reported in
news programs.

F. KBUY-FM (Fort Worth):

KBUY-FM will employ a minimum of one Mexican-American
full-time announcer, which announcer will be heard regularly
on the air. This announcer will be hired no later than September 15, 1971.

Further, KBUY-FM will employ a minimum of one full-time
Mexican-American news reporter, which reporter will have
a primary responsibility for covering news items of, about,
and of interest to the Mexican-American community within
KBUY-FM's primary broadcasting area. This reporter will
be hired no later than June 15, 1971.

By June 1, 1972, at least one-half of KBUY-FM's full-time on-
the-air staff will be Mexican-American.

Notification of existing job and job-training vacancies at the
station will be broadcast by KBUY-FM on weekdays during
the hours of 8 a.m. to 7 p.m. to advise Mexican-Americans
and others of those vacancies as they occur.

G. KXOL-AM (Fort Worth):

The station will broadcast notification of existing job vacancies
and will continue to employ blacks and Mexican-Americans
in proportion to their numbers in the local area.

Programming

A. McGraw-Hill:

Programming. MACs will suggest a coordinating committee
to work with McGraw-Hill in producing 18 La Raza programs
on Mexican-American culture and history in the four markets.
There will be 36 prime-time specials, 12 to be produced
locally over three years on minority cultural subjects, 12 on
achievements, interests, and problems of Chicanos, and 12
on blacks.

B. Doubleday:

Programming. Specific agreements to present a fair and bal-
anced view of Chicanos include four half-hour, prime-time
specials in 1973 and 1974, 30 minutes of prime time in the
period ending July 31, 1973, and 180 minutes per year in 1973
and 1974. All stations will carry public service announcements and will produce and carry six programs on local
matters to be offered to other stations at cost. A survey of
the market of available programming will be made, advertisements demeaning to the Chicano deleted, and compensation
made on an equal basis when outside staff is used. No one
with a Spanish accent will be barred from speaking on any
station. Chicanos will be advised of any network programs
concerning them. When assessing the public service value
of a Chicano program, ratings will be taken considering the
language barrier and, when necessary, the survey will be in
Spanish.

C. Combined Communications:

KBTV-TV (Denver). (a) Children's programming will be en-
larged by a series of locally produced, regularly scheduled
programs. (b) The program "Channel 9 File" will deal once
a month specifically with minority needs and interests on
topics suggested by the task force. (c) The task force may
bring to CCC's attention noteworthy programs or issues that
are susceptible to broadcast in Spanish and, if approved, will
be aired.

KARK-TV (Little Rock). (a) News events in black communities
will be covered. (b) Diverse views on controversial matters
will be presented. KARK will actively seek diverse views
that exist within the black community. The public right to
present opposing views will be regularly announced. (c)
Three programs—"Contact," "Little Rock Today," and "Challenge 71"—will inform the public about the problems of

poverty and the steps being taken to alleviate it. The programs will publicize the rights of poor persons to obtain services.

D. KTRK-AM-FM (Houston):
KTRK will attempt to find programs in Spanish for non-English-speaking audiences. It will do special reports on minority problems.

E. KQEO-AM (Albuquerque):
The station will give consideration to the broadcasting of music of special interest to the Chicano community; the station will continue to broadcast "Youth Speaks Out," an hour-long, local public-affairs program, and to consider program topics suggested by CEETRUTH; the station will continue "The Chicano in Albuquerque," begun in September in cooperation with Alianza Federal de Pueblos Libres, or find a suitable substitute in consultation with minority groups. The station promises to include Catholic-oriented content in its religious programming.

F. KOA-TV-AM-FM (Denver):
In response to the needs identified, KOA-TV will offer a half-hour weekly program for 26 weeks, consisting of 13 initial programs with option to continue by mutual consent. It is anticipated that the program will be scheduled on Saturday or Sunday afternoon. The committee will arrange for and supply the program content and talent, drawing from the Spanish-surnamed community for a diverse range of subject matter, including news, informational material, and entertainment. Recognizing the diversity of possible interests desiring access, all groups and interests will be represented.
The station will provide air time, studio facilities for live production, videotape, taping time, and the technical staff necessary to produce the program.

G. KBUY-FM (Fort Worth):
When, and as feasible, set up an on-the-job training program for a Mexican-American who is a resident of KBUY-FM's primary broadcasting area. KBUY-FM will broadcast daily (Monday through Friday) between the hours of 8 a.m. and 7 p.m. public affairs and/or educational programming directed to the Spanish-speaking community. Initially, it is contemplated that the program will be one hour in length.

KBUY-FM will present programs that will probe the educational
problems and potentialities of the Dallas-Fort Worth area,
subject to the availability of such programs.

KBUY-FM will carry religious programming representative
of the populace in KBUY-FM's primary broadcasting area,
subject to the availability of such programs.

KBUY-FM will seek to broaden its coverage of significant news
events, both on the national and regional scenes and in the
local Mexican-American community.

Also, KBUY-FM will designate one person on its program staff
to be responsible for developing and coordinating local, network, and syndicated public affairs and educational programming of the type described later in this statement. This person will be designated no later than July 15, 1971.

H. KXOL-AM (Fort Worth):

Two new programs will be broadcast weekly covering poverty
and economic development, the heritage and culture of minority groups and in-depth coverage of controversial issues.

KXOL will inquire into the various aid programs, such as welfare, and, specifically, how they benefit minorities. Findings
will be broadcast on "Fort Worth Wants to Know."

Minority Businesses

A. McGraw-Hill:

Assistance to Minority Businessmen. McGraw-Hill plans
"know-how" panels, featuring experts, for minority businessmen in local markets and will assist in improving the com-
petence of minority businessmen, especially in management,
marketing, and promotion. Stations will also be encouraged
to use the products and services of minorities.

B. Doubleday:

Promotion of Chicano Businessmen. News and features will
be done on the opening of new Chicano businesses and opportunities given for bidding for furnishing services, supplies,
etc. Advertisements will be made in Spanish-language papers
for job openings; program promotion and advertisements for
federal contracts and programs will be included on the radio.

C. KOA-TV-AM-FM (Denver):

The station will permit the Colorado Committee to secure
contributing sponsorships, at rates to be mutually agreed

upon, from Spanish-surnamed businesses to provide a forum for emerging enterprises. Proceeds from such contributors will be used to underwrite the costs of producing a weekly half-hour program. Sponsor participation will be handled on the air as interviews or direct statements relating to the business and its products and services; if regular locally produced commercials are desired, they will be made available on the same terms and conditions applicable to all advertisers.

Scholarships

A. Doubleday:

Beginning with the fall, 1972 semester, $5,000 annually will be available to the Corporate Advisory Committee to divide among the four cities, to include all areas of radio-television broadcasting, including management. Recipients will also be given part-time employment and Doubleday will guarantee 500 hours per year of training or employment to scholarship recipients.

B. KQEO-AM (Albuquerque):

The station will provide a scholarship for a minority group student and supplement it with part-time employment at the station to train him for broadcast work.

C. KBUY-FM (Fort Worth):

KBUY-FM will set up at least one scholarship of $150 for a Mexican-American student who resides in KBUY-FM's primary broadcasting area to go to an accredited school of broadcasting. This scholarship will be granted yearly.

D. KXOL-AM (Fort Worth):

KXOL has established a scholarship at Texas Christian University. A black student now is the recipient.

Sensitivity Training

A. Doubleday:

Doubleday and local stations will require key personnel to participate in sensitivity training designed to provide them with greater insight into and understanding of the Chicano community.

B. Combined Communications:
    CCC will evaluate and select sensitivity training courses and will pay the reasonable costs thereof. The task force will be consulted in the selection process.

C. KXOL-AM (Fort Worth):
    Station agrees to urge staff attendance at sensitivity sessions.

Public-Service Announcements

A. McGraw-Hill:
    This relatively new provision commits time for one-minute public-access, public-service announcements by local people and groups. The station will decide which will be broadcast but cannot reject a message because it is controversial. Any script accompanied by a petition with 100 names must be considered.

B. KTRK-AM-FM (Houston):
    More PSAs will be produced in Spanish in order to inform non-English-speaking people about community health, education, and transportation services.

C. KQEO-AM (Albuquerque):
    The station will prepare announcements, program featurettes, feature news stories, and promotional public-service activities for local minority information programs. In these efforts, both the Chicano newsman and CEETRUTH will provide an advisory insight into area problems worthy of coverage.

D. KBUY-AM (Fort Worth):
    The station will actively solicit public-service announcements from local groups and organizations. In addition to other appropriate means, an announcement will be made daily, between the hours of 8 a.m. and 7 p.m., soliciting public-service announcements.

E. KXOL-AM (Fort Worth):
    The station will make announcements five times daily soliciting public-service announcements.

Minority Training

A. <u>McGraw-Hill</u>:
McGraw-Hill will select and provide training each year for three minority persons in each of the three larger markets and two minority persons in Bakersfield. Persons who successfully complete their training program will be hired if appropriate employment openings are available.

B. <u>Doubleday</u>:
Recipients of scholarships provided for in this agreement will be guaranteed 500 hours per year of training or employment.

C. <u>KQEO-AM</u> (Albuquerque):
The station will train one minority group student for broadcast work.

D. <u>KARK-TV</u> (Little Rock):
As the needs arise, KARK will train black personnel at all job levels. It will look to the advisory council as its primary source of recruitment.

E. <u>KOA-TV-AM-FM</u> (Denver):
An individual will be selected for broadcast training by KOA-TV in conjunction with and under the funding provisions of the Jobs for Progress program. This individual will be responsible for coordinating details of the aforementioned TV program and will be given other on-the-job learning assignments throughout the duration of the training project.

F. <u>KBUY-FM</u> (Fort Worth):
In a continuing pursuit of its goal of providing truly equal opportunity for all, KBUY-FM will set up training programs to encourage and assist minority persons, especially Mexican-Americans, in obtaining the skills prerequisite to securing employment in all facets of the broadcast industry.

NOTES

1. "6 Chicanos File Complaint with FCC Re KVOU 'Unresponsiveness' to Needs," Variety, October 7, 1970, p. 24.
2. "Renewal Battles in the Rockies," Broadcasting March 8, 1971, p. 32.

3. "Signs of Changing Times in Renewals," Broadcasting, May 17, 1971, p. 34.

4. "Charges Untrue, WOAI-TV Answers," Broadcasting, Septembem 6, 1971, p. 32.

5. "Ethnic Dispute in San Antonio," Broadcasting, July 5, 1971, p. 28.

6. "FCC Rejects Challenges in San Antonio, Buffalo," Broadcasting, November 27, 1972, p. 8.

7. "Inch by Inch, FCC Moves Ahead on Renewal Cases," Broadcasting, November 13, 1972, p. 25.

8. "The Media," Broadcasting, July 12, 1971, p. 33.

9. "Enter the Alianza in Renewal Attacks," Broadcasting, August 23, 1971, p. 34.

10. "Challengers Seek Station Figures," Broadcasting, July 26, 1971, p. 21.

11. "Federal Agency Rulings," Law Week, September 14, 1971, p. 2133.

12. "Enter the Alianza in Renewal Attacks," p. 35.

13. "Open Season on Texas Stations," Broadcasting, August 9, 1971, p. 19.

14. "Closed Circuit," Broadcasting, August 30, 1971, p. 7.

15. "Minorities Gang Up in Albuquerque," Broadcasting, September 6, 1971, p. 33.

16. Leonard Zeidenberg, "The Struggle over Broadcast Access," Broadcasting, September 20 1971, p. 34.

17. "Catchword in California Renewals: Minorities," Broadcasting, November 8, 1971, p. 42.

18. Ibid., p. 43.

19. Ibid.

20. Joaquin Montemayor, letter to Julian Klugman (CRS Western Regional Director), July 29, 1971.

21. Washington Evening Star, April 20, 1972.

22. "8 Challenged Stations Win Renewals from FCC," Broadcasting, January 1, 1973, p. 6.

23. "Diverse Appeals to D.C. Court," Broadcasting, July 3, 1972, p. 23.

24. "Hard Bargains for KQEO too," Broadcasting, November 29, 1971, p. 58.

25. "KEST Strikes Bargain with Citizen Group," Broadcasting, March 13, 1972, p. 35.

26. Zeidenberg, "The Struggle over Broadcast Access," p. 37.

27. San Francisco Chronicle, April 21, 1972.

28. "McGraw-Hill Sets Record for Concessions to Minorities," Broadcasting, May 15, 1972, p. 25.

29. Ibid.

30. Ibid., p. 26.

6

IMPLEMENTATION OF
THE AGREEMENTS

Generalizations about the long-range effects of the agreements are difficult to make, but it seems certain that they will have a tremendous effect on the entire Southwest. It is even too soon to tell how the agreements are being implemented in the multitude of communities being affected. The Community Relations Service's communication section was about to launch into an analysis of the implementation of the various contracts, but the section was disbanded before the project could get started.

This section will deal with two specific cases in which the broadcaster-Chicano agreements have been under way for several months. The first is the story of a Mexican-American reporter hired by WBAP-TV-AM-FM, Dallas-Fort Worth. The second case is a study of the implementation of the Doubleday Broadcasting agreement with Chicanos in El Paso, Texas.

I AM A REPORTER

When Henry de la Garza began covering Chicano affairs as the first Mexican-American broadcast reporter in the Dallas-Fort Worth area in June 1971 he was met with a combination of skepticism and hostility from both fellow journalists and Chicanos. He is one of many new Chicano reporters who are finding that in order to serve their employers and their people they must learn to walk a tightrope. One of the first questions asked of him by the Chicano activists was whether he was a Chicano or a Mexican-American, meaning, was he sympathetic to la causa? His answer: "I am a professional reporter first."[1] The answer was not what the activist would have liked, but as de la Garza has learned in the time since the question was asked, being objective is the only way for a Chicano reporter to maintain his job and his professional credibility.

De la Garza graduated from the University of Texas at El Paso with a B.A. in journalism in 1971 and took the broadcasting job immediately after graduation. At the time, WBAP was involved in negotiations with the Coalition for the Free Flow of Information (CFFI) and he was hired, he suspects, because of the agreement that seemed imminent. Because he comes from an upper-middle-class background, he went to schools in El Paso that were predominantly attended by Anglos and therefore speaks little Spanish. He admits that his involvement in, or sympathy toward, the Chicano Movement was never too great, but that the attitude of the media in his new job has caused a reaction in him.

Anglo reporters in the Dallas-Fort Worth area were openly hostile when he was first hired because they felt that other, more qualified reporters, could not compete against someone who was hired solely on the basis of ethnic background. Some told him that "this minority thing is only temporary" and that "minorities will eventually flounder from inexperience and finally withdraw, and then the broadcasting business will return to normal."[2]

One 13-year veteran film editor and newscast producer asked de la Garza if he really believed that he would be around "five years from now." The answer? "How the hell should I know?! After all, they never gave me any assurances when I was hired that even you would be around five years from now."

As his first beat, he was assigned to cover city hall for three months and was then switched to minority activities. Today, he is actually a general assignment reporter with an emphasis on minorities, and his anger at the initial hostility that he encountered has sparked his desire to prove himself as a reporter and has stirred his pride in being a Mexican-American. He feels that he has helped the station in its ability to give deeper coverage of minority activities, which he believes has improved tremendously:

> People are seeing themselves on TV now. They never even saw a TV camera on the North Side before. Now, if there is a rally, we know about it. They let us know. Chicano activists come into the studio regularly with news releases; this is something they never did before. They are also getting more professional.[3]

The reaction of the Mexican-American community was also mixed at first. The activists were hostile, while the established Mexican-Americans "treat me like gold. They are very proud." His first encounter with Chicano militants is a story worth repeating:

I can recall covering my first La Raza Unida news story—
a voter registration seminar on the city's South Side.
Arriving in my well-marked news unit, I quickly introduced myself to the Chicano leaders, and then began setting up my camera and lights. Suddenly, one of them
called me over and asked me why I wanted to cover their
seminar. I frankly explained that our news had not
covered La Raza in some time, that I was there to give
them equal time, and that, if they didn't want the free
coverage, I could find other stories to report instead.
Apparently, my response seemed to satisfy the mustachioed brown-beret because we have become good
friends since and have worked closely in covering the
political activities of Texas' third political party in Fort
Worth.[4]

Minority coverage since the agreement that indirectly led to
his being hired is summed up this way by de la Garza:

As far as coverage of minority news events by minority
newsmen goes, one thing is definite. Obviously, the
coverage is expanding . . . but it is also becoming more
in-depth. Boycott marches, the 16th of September, and
La Raza used to be just news which happened, and that's
as much as people ever were told. Now, people are told
what events led up to the boycott march. Now, they are
told more than a Mexico's Independence Day parade wound
its way through downtown, but that the parade sponsors
are trying to make the activity relevant to today's
Chicano Movement. Now they are exposed to La Raza
organizers so often that the brown-beret leaders are almost household names, and their goals are dinner topics
in many unexpected homes.[5]

Similar effects have been noticed in other cities where broadcaster-Chicano agreements have been implemented. In El Paso,
Texas, a city of 350,000, where Mexican-Americans slightly outnumber
the Anglo population, the effects have not been quite as dramatic,
because of the fact that some Mexican-Americans were employed as
newspaper reporters prior to the pressures of the Chicano Movement.
However, even in that city, there were no Mexican-Americans working
as on-camera newsmen for any of the three television stations before
the media became a local issue for Chicanos. Then, as the challenge
of KROD-TV (the local Doubleday station) got under way, there suddenly appeared on each station at least one Mexican-American

newsman. So, even though the legal agreement was only with the one station, it seems as if other broadcasters felt enough pressure to cause them to instigate action on their own. At KROD there were no Mexican-American newsmen prior to the challenge, although there were Mexican-Americans working in a variety of other jobs.[6] After the agreement, the number of Mexican-Americans increased by about 20 percent, including two on-camera newsmen, two cameramen, a director, an engineer, the head of the film department, an assistant promotion manager, three girls in traffic, two maintenance men, and some typists. Thus, there were some very visible and immediate changes brought about by the challenging groups as both direct and indirect consequences of the negotiated agreement. But long-range effects are still difficult to measure, and may vary greatly from city to city. Therefore, the following discussion of the implementation of the Doubleday agreement in El Paso cannot be taken as a valid measurement of how the agreements are faring, but only as one case study.

THE DOUBLEDAY AGREEMENT

The Committee for the Development of Mass Communications in El Paso is a combination of an old committee of the same name and the Committee for the Development of Mass Communications on Unity and Action. The two former committees both represented El Paso in the original structuring of the Doubleday contract; afterwards, they reformed into a single group to implement the agreement with KROD-TV. The committee is composed of representatives of all Chicano organizations in El Paso. However, the bulk of its work is conducted under the supervision of the Local Advisory Committee, a seven-man board elected by the committee at large. Meetings of the Local Advisory Committee are generally scheduled once a week, during the evening hours, since most of the members are employed full time during the day. Additionally, John Siqueiros, chairman of the Radio and Television Department, University of Texas at El Paso, serves as an advisor to the committee. He has a B.A. in broadcasting from the University of Texas at El Paso and has served 21 years in the broadcasting business, including positions as general manager of several Doubleday broadcasting properties. Humberto Hernandez, former chairman of the committee, believes that Siqueiros's advice has been invaluable, especially in the beginning when the committee was unaware of the many intricacies of broadcasting and often was lost in the technical jargon used by broadcasters.[7]

Following the letter of the contract, the committee is supposed to meet once each month with the local station representatives; however, to a great extent, the initial distrust of both sides has dissipated

130

and a more informal arrangement, which both parties find more satisfactory, has been worked out. This arrangement utilizes Hernandez
as a focal point and liaison between the committee and KROD-TV.
This enables Hernandez to exercise his judgment on issues and difficulties as they arise. Jerry Rose, KROD program director, explained
the workability of this method. "If Bert wasn't able to work like this,
it might take ten years to produce a half-hour film."[8] This statement
refers to Hernandez's role as producer of the first film called for in
the contract. Additionally, he was the committee's representative to
the June 1972 meeting of the Corporate Advisory Committee in Odessa.

Ascertainment

Ascertainment had not begun at the time of the study; however,
Edward M. Sleighel, general manager of KROD, said that a professional ascertainment company will probably conduct the process,
supplemented by advice from the committee and interviews conducted
by himself, Jerry Rose, and Marlin Haines, the news director.

Employment

Prior to the contract signing, eight Chicanos were employed at
KROD. Since that time seven additional Chicanos and one black have
been hired, but during the latter period two Chicanos have left to
accept other positions. The most recent hiring was of a young Chicano,
six credit hours short of graduation from UCLA, majoring in the
psychology of mass communications. His position is cameraman,
the only position available at the time of his hiring. A Chicano anchors
a daily news program, as specified in the contract. He also serves
as a reporter.

Sensitivity Training

A program in sensitivity training has been devised but not yet
executed. There is no great rush on either part to begin the sessions
because it is felt that other conditions of the contract require a higher
priority. This is largely due to what Chicanos feel is an increased
sensitivity of the KROD staff as a result of their first film production.
As Hernandez said, "In producing the first special, I sensitized most
of the people on the staff."[9]

Scholarships

This first scholarship board met and chose three scholarship recipients, all of whom attend the University of Texas at El Paso. El Paso's $1,250 share of the annual scholarship fund was divided equally among the three students.

Programming

The first prime-time special, a documentary called "Chicano in Transition," was aired by KROD on two separate occasions as a result of the favorable audience reaction after the first showing. A local radio station used its morning call-in show for two days after the first airing to allow its listeners to discuss the documentary. The film was produced by the Chicano committee with technical assistance from the station. Two members of the committee were paid by the station on an hourly basis during the production of the film, while others volunteered their time. Generally, the results of the talk-show discussions indicated that the program was well-received by the community, many of whom praised the show for its technical expertise. In fact, those involved with the production were surprised at the quality of the final product. Cindy Webber, a graduate of Stanford's School of Cinematography, and the only KROD staff member with documentary experience, said that at first she believed the project was too ambitious because it attempted to cover too much at once.[10] The program was an overview of Chicano culture, art, education, economic development, and politics, with special attention to the Chicanos' relationship to the city of El Paso. Furthermore, Miss Webber felt that the Chicanos' lack of technical and professional expertise would seriously affect the outcome of the film. None of the Chicano group members had any film experience. Other staff members voiced similar opinions, but when the documentary was completed and on the air, the reaction was summed up by Jerry Rose: "It was a good program."[11] The fact that the management volunteered to air the program a second time is an indication that the program caused considerable goodwill in the community toward the station.

The production of the second and third films of the series, however, has run into problems. One will concentrate on the education of the Chicano and the other on Chicano culture and art, but much of the group's energy has been expended and the second film is far behind schedule. Other effects on programming have included more coverage of Mexican-American problems and affairs, as well as special programs, such as "4 Noon," a weekday talk show, and a Sunday morning show entitled "Nuestra Hora" (Our Hour), which alternates between two Chicano groups. Every other week the program is called "<u>Perspectiva</u>" (Perspective), when it is hosted by the second organization.

One Public-service announcement was completed. It spoke of the opening of a public El Paso Conference on Elementary and Secondary Education sponsored by the El Paso Educational Research Project, an equality-in-education-oriented program.

Conclusion: Problems and Successes

The problems encountered in this effort are not new to minority organizations. Lack of time, money, and personnel are the foremost enemies.

The problem of money at times seems insurmountable. Doubleday has paid for the filming and scholarships, but the costs of even such small, but critical, items as postage and paper must usually be borne at personal expense or begged and borrowed from friends. Consequently, the entire effort, and especially the dissemination of information, is handicapped.

There are no costs for labor because there are no funds. Hernandez was a Robert F. Kennedy Fellow until June 1973 and, of necessity, much of his time is devoted to other projects. He has no broadcasting background; consequently, his training is on an "as the problems arise" basis and inevitably mistakes are made that are only recognized after the damage. Wasted time and effort are common maladies of inexperience. Hernandez explains, "if only one trained and sensitive person could devote full time to the implementation of the contract, the already favorable results would greatly increase."[12]

He goes on to explain that "one of the basic problems of implementing the contract to its fullest extent is the lack of time that can be devoted to the project by the committee members because of their economic conditions." That is, they are working people and students, which allows them only a little time each week to contribute to committee objectives.

Some specific problems and disagreements exist. Many committee members feel that the Chicano newsmen hired by the station, while not a negative force, lack a positive approach to the needs of the <u>barrio</u> Chicano. Some resented the refusal to hire a committee-referred Chicano with a master's degree in mass communications because of his lack of news-writing experience. They feel that perhaps he should have been offered on-the-job training and that the station lacks affirmative action in this respect.

For the most part, however, the "greatest problem" has been conquered. As Edward Sleighel said, "in the beginning the greatest problem can be narrowed down to one word—communication. But now Bert knows that if he has a problem he can pick up a phone and call me and we'll do our best to work it out."[13] Hernandez agrees, "if we need something, I just call Sleighel or Jerry [Rose]."

Communication between KROD and the Chicano community has been established; now the business of communicating to the public is beginning.

NOTES

1. Henry de la Garza, private interview held in El Paso, Tex., September 20, 1972.

2. The Prospector (The University of Texas at El Paso student newspaper), September 28, 1972.

3. De la Garza, interview, September 20, 1972.

4. Ibid.

5. Ibid.

6. Edward M. Sleighel, private interview held in El Paso, Tex., May 12, 1973.

7. Humberto Hernandez, private interview held in El Paso, Tex., November 10, 1972. (The interviews with Hernandez, Rose, and Webber were conducted by Joe Quintana, journalism student at the University of Texas at El Paso.)

8. Jerry Rose, private interview held in El Paso, Tex., November 17, 1972.

9. Hernandez, interview, November 10, 1972.

10. Cindy Webber, private interview held in El Paso, Tex., November 17, 1972.

11. Rose, interview, November 17, 1972.

12. Hernandez, interview, November 10, 1972.

13. Sleighel, interview, May 12, 1973.

Public access to the media is not desired only by minority groups
and radicals. It is a problem that confronts anyone who has something
controversial to say to the mass audience and who finds it impossible
to get his message across. This phenomenon has been discovered by
poor and rich alike, in cases where the nature of the message is controversial or contrary to the powers that control the mass media.
When a group of white businessmen wanted to speak out against the
war in Vietnam, they approached WTOP-TV in Washington, D.C., with
money in hand to buy air time. The station refused to sell it to them.
The same thing has happened to U.S. congressmen, political candidates,
right-wing groups, left-wing groups, as well as minority groups. And,
in May 1973, the Supreme Court ruled that radio and TV stations have
an absolute right to refuse to sell air time for advertisements dealing
with political campaigns or controversial public issues.[1] In such a
system, in which the channels of communication are effectively closed
to the public, devious means for gaining access are often employed.
Thus the need for the sit-in, the demonstration, the riot, the march,
the license challenge, and sometimes violence. These are the extents
to which citizens have gone to inform others of their cause. They are
attempts by the public, or special publics, to share in the power of the
media. As FCC Commissioner Nicholas Johnson says, "Information
is power. People will act if they are informed."[2] But without the
means of communicating that information, no group can establish a
solid power base from which to grow. This, then, is the crux of the
battle that has up to now been focused on the broadcast media. It is
essentially a battle between the haves and the have nots—those who
have the power to communicate and inform and those who do not.

Due to the nature of the technology, the fight has been caused,
for the most part, by the scarcity of channels available for communicating in broadcasting and by the high costs of starting a daily

metropolitan newspaper. But now that the unlimited channel capacity of Community Antenna Television (CATV) is becoming a reality in major urban areas, it is possible that this limitation will be lifted once and for all, allowing everyone and anyone the opportunity to be heard. On this premise, and on the existing agreements with broadcasters, rest the hopes of the powerless.

Cable television may have the greatest potential for social reform of any medium, yet its introduction into our system is already beginning to resemble, historically, the growth of broadcasting which led to the present dilemma. Ownership of CATV systems is quickly falling into the hands of a few private, white entrepreneurs, with the Federal Communications Commission playing referee between the big-money holders—and the public merely being paid lip service. At least, this is the scene as viewed by those who are self-appointed guardians of the public interest. Indeed, the data on CATV tend to bear out this concern. In a 20-year period from 1950 to 1970, the number of CATV systems jumped from 70 to 2,570 and the number of total subscribers grew from 14,000 to 5,300,000.[3] By early 1973, there were nearly 6,000,000 subscribers.[4] The top ten cable companies accounted for 1,760,590 subscribers[5] in 1970 and the number continues to grow, with TelePrompTer Corporation, Cox Cable Communications, Inc., and American Television and Communications Corporation leading the pack. More than 50 percent of the cable systems in March 1970 were owned by large communication companies, with broadcasters owning 36.5 percent, newspaper-publishing companies owning 8.2 percent, and phone companies owning 5.8 percent.[6]

At the local level, the battles are being waged furiously, with 10 to 20 groups sometimes involved. The situation has become acute since the FCC lifted its freeze on urban cablecasting in April 1972[7]; 206 new systems were approved by the FCC by April 1973.[8]

Things have happened so fast that few communities have stopped to think about the far-reaching monopolistic implications of awarding an exclusive franchise to a single cable company, and even fewer voters are well-informed enough to be able to make sound decisions about this overwhelmingly complex subject. As a result, there are few communities with publicly or city-owned cable companies and no such arrangement exists in a major market. This is in spite of the fact that cities are in constant financial difficulty and cablecasting promises to be extremely profitable in a very short amount of time. According to Department of Justice figures, a cable operator in a city of 450,000 (where most of the franchises have yet to be let) will invest about $10.5 million, but realize a profit in just five years with gross revenues totaling $11.3 million.[9]

The rush for control of cable television is progressing without much real knowledge of how cablecasting will affect society in general, or programming in particular. But few have doubts about its potential power and many have ideas on how it can be put to use. Charles Tate, in his introduction to a minority handbook on CATV, visualizes the cable as the solution to many of the problems of the poor:

> It is this system (CATV) that could enable America's minorities to challenge the communication systems that exploit the ghettoes, barrios, and reservations. Control, ownership, and operation of cable systems by minorities could provide economic and political leverage, and the management and technical expertise required to accomplish a dramatic break in the cycle of dependency and exploitation.
>
> Imagine television and radio systems where blacks could program for blacks, Chicanos for Chicanos, Indians for Indians, and Puerto Ricans for Puerto Ricans—a system that can give the community a communications voice as well as the income and profit that the system receives for providing this service.[10]

The high hopes for public service advantages of CATV center around two essential elements: first, the cable will provide an almost unlimited number of channels (24-60 is now about as high as any go), and second, the cable makes it economically possible to program to small audiences.[11] (With commercial broadcasting, a person or group must pay the high rates dictated by the few channels directed at the mass audiences.) In addition to providing more and clearer channels, the cable can supply educational services, localized neighborhood programming, two-way communication, televised public meetings, free or very cheap political campaigning, store-front public-access studios, shopping services, banking services, automatic home fire and burglar alarm systems, and library retrieval of information, to list only a few possibilities. But, warns the Office of Communication of the United Church of Christ, "Cable is in danger of being pre-empted by commercial operators more interested in profit than in public service."[12] It is with this warning in mind that the issue of public access to cable, particularly with respect to minorities, must be discussed.

PUBLIC-ACCESS CHANNELS

At the heart of the public-service issue are two critical matters: the use of public-access channels and the control and ownership of CATV systems by the public. It is here that much of the hope lies for the solution of the economic, educational, and political problems of minorities. The latter is far from becoming a reality, while the first is already a reality in a few areas and is destined to become widespread when the FCC's March 1972 rule made such channels mandatory. In a letter addressed to the chairmen of the House and Senate Subcommittees on Communication, FCC Chairman Dean Burch spelled out the details of FCC cable regulations, which were adopted in March 1972:

> . . . we will require that there be one free, dedicated, non-commercial, public-access channel available at all times on a non-discriminatory basis. . . . The public-access (soap box) channels are to be available on a first-come, first-served basis and without local censorship or prior restraint other than to preclude advertising, lotteries, or obscene or indecent matter.[13]

The rule affects different cable systems in different ways. Those franchises that were awarded prior to the March 1972 ruling were granted a delay in complying with the rule until 1977. Contracts awarded after the ruling must include provisions for immediate installation of public-access channels. In addition, the FCC will require that one channel be given to the city government and one provided for education purposes. In those few cities where public-access channels are activated, the enormous problems involved in their implementation have become evident. The Sloan Commission on Cable Communication discovered many of these problems and outlined them in their report. Some of these included how time is to be allotted, the procedure for sharing the most favorable time slots, dealing with unpopular opinions, dealing with those who would try to incite to riot or sedition, invasion of privacy, and violation of libel laws.[14]

Another factor that may prove to be an issue is the question of cost to the public for the use of the channels. Even though the channels will be "free" to the public, someone must absorb the cost of production. "Hopefully," said Dean Burch, "colleges and universities, high schools, recreation departments, churches, unions, and other community sources will have low-cost videotaping equipment available to the public. Whatever sources are available, however, we will require that the cable operator maintain at least minimal production facilities for public use within the franchise area."[15] The cable operator will be required to make such facilities available without charge for "brief live studio presentations not exceeding five minutes in duration," but could make charges for production services to groups wishing to use the public-access channel for longer and more complex presentations.[16] The obvious issue raised here is whether or not five minutes is enough time to present a view, and, if more time is needed, who will foot the bill and how much will the bill be? These questions are far from being settled and may eventually be left up to the individual community to determine.

Once the details of how the channels are to be utilized logistically are settled, then the problem of the composition of the program remains. Two theories of programming, outlined by the United Church of Christ, are already being implemented to a limited extent in some communities. Both theories stem from the idea that public-access programming should have a unique local quality. The first school of cable producers favors what they call a "people's video" in which programming in the traditional sense of fully produced television "shows" is dispensed with completely. Instead, they substitute what they call "direct communication" materials provided by the local population. These materials take the form of videotapes made in the streets, at local meetings, or in door-to-door interviews.[17] This theory centers around the use of economical portable videotaping equipment (portapaks), which are used as direct communication bridges between people and as tools for community organizing. A complete portapak consisting of video camera, tape unit, built-in microphone, and monitor sells for about $1,500 and is extremely simple to operate. Using this type of equipment, any group or individual can illustrate its problem in a homemade documentary with sound and with a reproduction quality that is suitable for cablecasting.

The second school of programmers believes that such programming will be too unprofessional to attract much of an audience. This school wants to interest people in community problems by using traditional methods of television production with more sophisticated techniques. Although it is more expensive, advocates of this theory say it is necessary, because public-access channels will be in direct competition with professionally produced programs.[18]

One of the few places where public-access channels are already operating is in New York City, where public access was a reality even before the FCC rules. The two cable operators have each set aside two channels for 24-hour public use on a first-come, first-serve basis.[19]

The diversity of the groups seeking access on these channels has ranged from the Prisoner's Solidarity Committee to the Boy Scouts. Much of the success of such presentations is credited to the Alternate Media Center, a public-interest organization which is showing community groups how to prepare programs for cable TV. The center is associated with the New York University School of the Arts and has been working with groups around the country, offering technical assistance in this new form of communication. Their method of operations consists of setting up workshops for the residents of a community to encourage people to get together to stimulate ideas and ultimately to decide on what they want to put on the cable. The Alternate Media Center was founded on the first theory of programming: that community groups are taught the use of the equipment and allowed to tell their stories in their own style with little supervision. Since its inception, the center has produced a large library of videotapes on community issues, which are available for use elsewhere in the country.[20]

In 1971, another group was organized to help with cable productions; this group adhered to the second theory. Open Channel is a nonprofit, foundation-funded entity with the goal of providing technical assistance and training, as well as technical resources, to groups that want to use the public channels. They get help from a pool of professional producers, directors, writers, and cameramen who donate their time and expertise to help the public produce their programs. Among the more than eighty organizations Open Channel has worked with are the Museum of Modern Art, the Puerto Rican Dance Theater, and the Inwood Advocate, a community newspaper. This organization can produce a one-hour program for as little as $600.[21]

Chicago is another area that is quickly gaining experience in public-access programming, using both programming models, in spite of the fact that the city is not yet wired for cable. Community Programs, Inc. is a Chicago-based nonprofit, management consulting firm that specializes in communications and lists an association of settlement houses among its biggest clients.[22] The organization is trying to use videotape to bring the goals of social-service agencies more in line with the needs of the communities they serve. In consultation with its client agency, Community Programs selects a community organization with which to work, it goes in with portapaks to document the problem, edit the tape, and show it to the client agency in an effort to try to get the agency to listen to its constituency. "With video," says originator Ted William Theodore, "we can end the 'those people' syndrome by showing there is a commonality to all people—that a welfare mother is not so different from the wife of an executive in what she wants for her kids."[23] He hopes that the people in the community will learn to look to cable as a way of making their needs known.

Meanwhile, a political science instructor at the University of Illinois, Chicago Circle Campus, Kaye Miller, is using video tape units operated by student crews in an attempt to stimulate widespread half-inch tape use through two poor sections of the city. In the uptown neighborhood, Miller worked with the Young Patriots in an effort to build support for a proposed health-care clinic. Through video tape they hope to attract outside resources to their project. In another section, Miller works with welfare recipients in order to "develop a dialectic between the felt needs and the objective needs of the people.

The point is to try to involve them in a process through which they can discover what their needs really are and develop organizational skills with which to work toward affecting them." Although he doesn't see public-access channels as the solution to all the problems, Miller sees a need for enabling people to take advantage of the opportunity: "Only by making sure there is a lot of equipment out there for people to use in their own way will we have any chance of preventing cable from becoming a repetition of today's bullshit television."[24]

Two other groups working in video tape communication in Chicago are Imedia and Videopolis. The first is a videotape production center that provides tapes on a contract basis to anyone except "the fascist community." Richard Stromberg, one of the company members, explains how his group adheres to the second programming theory:

> We consider communications to be an art. No matter how good the content, if production values aren't up to par, nobody will care. Our idea is to raise the production values of groups interested in eventually using the public-access channels. We'll do the work for them. There's no need for people to buy specialized television equipment, much less to learn how to use it.[25]

Videopolis is a community video-access center that wants to nourish a public demand for use of public access by beginning to stimulate a wide variety of half-inch tape use in the community before the channels are available. David Meyers, one of the project coordinators, explains why his group is concerned:

> Experience has shown that cable companies play as small a role as possible in providing community services and encouraging access—since these aspects of their operation don't pay.[26]

Although Videopolis plans to concentrate its efforts on groups that are likely to develop their own ongoing video programs, the center hopes to serve all kinds of future programming needs of the community.

THE FRANCHISE PROBLEM

Community interest in cable television came too late in many areas to take advantage of the numerous benefits possible. Many cities and municipalities granted franchises containing no guarantee that the entire community would be wired, that an optimum number of channels would be made available, or that there would be public-

access channels. The 1972 FCC ruling has helped solve the problem
in the case of the public-access channels and has created three categories of cities: (1) Cities with franchises that were awarded prior
to March 1972 without guarantees of public-access channels. Cities
falling into this category are numerous and will not have public-access
channels until 1977, unless they can renegotiate the contracts. (2)
Cities with franchises that were awarded prior to the ruling, but which
required public-access channels as part of the contract. Very few
cities fall into this category, New York being the primary example.
(3) Cities that have not awarded franchises or have awarded them
after the rulings. Most major cities are in the process of awarding
franchises and all cities in this category will have public-access
channels upon activation of their systems. But in spite of the fact that
public-access channels seem a distant reality in some areas, the concept is spreading rapidly, since the courts have ruled that cable operators with 3,500 or more subscribers must operate "to a significant
extent as a local outlet" by originating their own programming in their
own production facilities.[27] The result has been that cablecasters
are so hard pressed for material that they are going into public-access
programming even before the channels become available. Unlike New
York, where public-access channels were written into the local franchise agreements, San Francisco cablecasters only have local origina-
tion to deal with. Typical of many cable operations, a small staff
with limited equipment has an entire channel to fill with programming.[28]

To do so, San Francisco Channel 6 takes its "Sony Rover" into
the streets once a week to tape "Videosketch," a show that attempts
to depict a true picture of daily life in the city without inflicting the
station's viewpoint. The station is training groups and individuals
in the use of the equipment and allowing them to make their own
shows. An example of this is a women's group that approached the
staff with a request for a women's liberation program. The production soon became a weekly program with the women taking large roles
in the technical production.

However, for the most part, the cable revolution has yet to
affect the average American, much less the resident of the ghetto,
the barrio, and the reservation. Even in San Francisco, where some
effort is being made by the cable owner to provide a touch of public
access where none is required by law, minorities are awakening to
the fact that they are not getting what they could be getting if they
had not been ignorant about CATV when franchises were granted. In
that city, Robert Gonzalez, a member of the city's 11-man board of
supervisors, called for a moratorium on further expansion of cable
in February 1973. He charged that the public was being denied access
to the only CATV operation in the city: TV Signal Corp., owned by
Viacom International, Inc. He also proposed that the seven-year-old

franchise held by Western Communications, Inc. be revoked because the system never has been built.[29]

Similar cries can be heard in many other communities where ignorant city officials and citizens have failed to provide for the public interest when the franchise was awarded. In Peoria, Illinois, a contract was signed as early as 1965 in a sealed-bid process with no public hearings, no citizen involvement, and no outside consultation. The agreement with General Electric Cablevision did not include specific performance requirements and six years later no cable had been installed in the city. In January 1971, the city's corporation counsel began an effort to force the company to make good its contract and eventually filed suit. But the courts held in favor of General Electric and the city still has no cable television.[30]

In direct contrast to this example is the experience in Oshkosh, Wisconsin, in which the city employed a consultant to draw up a model cable ordinance before bids were considered. As a result, Oshkosh now has a thirty-six channel cable system, in which two channels are reserved for municipal use and two for public access. In addition, the city has a separate two-way, twelve-channel "loop" interconnecting with the University of Wisconsin, all public and private schools, the Fox Valley Technical Institute, the library, and the museum for use in a community-wide curriculum development and teacher-training program.[31]

As the public and minorities are becoming aware that cable opportunities are slipping past them rapidly, haphazard groups and coalitions are being formed to get into action before it is too late. One such group nearly scored what would have been one of the most amazing access triumphs in history, if their contract with cablecasters had been fulfilled. A force of 16 minority organizations in California, calling themselves the Third World Coalition, reached an agreement with American Television & Communication Corporation and with Cox Cable Communications, Inc. which would have created a California network of cable channels for minorities.[32] The black and brown groups were to receive channels, equipment, and a minority training center, but the proposed merger between the two companies, around which the agreement was based, drew so much criticism that they decided not to merge and the deal fell through.

CHICANOS AND CABLE

As of late 1972, there were cable systems operating in all of the five Southwestern states, with California leading by far in the number of subscribers, with 834,615. Below are listed the Southwestern states, the number of subscribers and the number of communities being served in each state:[33]

143

California	1,656,000	391
Arizona	61,492	25
Colorado	54,354	42
New Mexico	54,373	42
Texas	359,257	232

Although the figures seem impressive, most of the cable systems operating are in the rural areas with few major Southwestern cities having cables in operation. In view of the fact that 80 percent of the Mexican-American population lives in the cities, it seems obvious that few are being reached by cable television. Cities in which cable franchises had not been awarded by May 1973 are Denver, Tucson, Los Angeles, Dallas, Phoenix, and Sacramento. Other cities, such as San Antonio and Albuquerque, have found themselves in the same situation as the city of Peoria. In San Antonio, the same company that holds the Peoria franchise, General Electric, was awarded the contract, and once again the company failed to wire the city for cable. As in many other similar situations, once the March 1972 FCC rules on signal importation were passed, the franchise-holder began making moves to lay the cable. Although a portion of the San Antonio contract is under renegotiation, the original contract provides for one public-access channel, six education channels, and one government channel to be put to use immediately upon activation of the system.[34] In addition, the city, in its recent renegotiation, has asked for and received two additional community channels for use by nonprofit groups who may wish to do their own programming. Production costs on these channels, other than free use of black and white video tape equipment, will be charged to the user, but the group may sell advertising to defray the expenses.

El Paso, Texas, has a cable system in operation that is owned by TelePrompTer, but the franchise was awarded without any provision for a public-access channel. Here, as in most other cities where franchises were awarded prior to the March 1972 FCC ruling, the cable operator is not obligated to provide such a channel until 1977. TelePrompTer has, however, made available to the city a channel of its own, as well as a channel for the public schools, one for the parochial schools, and one for the University of Texas at El Paso. None of these were in operation as of the summer of 1973.

In Albuquerque, New Mexico, a city-manager staff member, Gabrio Rodriguez, is busy working on amendments to the city's contract with the General Entertainment Company (a division of the Livingston Oil Company of Tulsa, Oklahoma), which has held the non-exclusive franchise for the city since 1968. The amendments would require the company to provide a public-access channel immediately upon activation of the system as well as to assist with production

144

costs. He is also working on setting up a regulatory body designed to deal with the cable system when it is installed.[35] The company is waiting for a "go-ahead" from the FCC on the importation of signals from other markets before it begins to lay its cable. The paperwork could take up to a year to process. In this case, as in other cases, local broadcasters have filed complaints that such importation would hurt them economically. Such complaints tend to delay cable installation, but current FCC trends indicate that such efforts will not stop the progress of cable into the cities.

California is probably the most sophisticated of the Southwestern states in communication and is also ahead in the area of public-access programming. David Green, program director for Bay Cablevision, Inc., in Berkeley, says that the staff of the company's local-origination channel persuaded the company to establish a public-access channel even though the franchise was awarded prior to the FCC ruling. Instead of giving only five minutes of air time, however, the channel will show almost any film brought in by a member of the community. They have not yet worked with any Chicano organization or group and have found that few people in the community take advantage of the new service.[36]

The two other public-access channels in operation in the Southwest are in Bakersfield and San Diego.

In spite of the excellent potential for Chicano access in the future, there is very little in the way of minority public-access programming being done now on cable in the Southwest. Mike Holland, regional director of the Cable Television Information Center (CTIC) in Washington, D.C., knew of only the two above-mentioned public-access channels being operated in any of the five Southwestern states, although there are examples of local-origination channels doing public-access programming.[37] The difference is that public-access channels are open to anyone at no expense for five minutes, while education channels, government channels, and local-origination channels are controlled by either a local institution or by the cable operator, making programming subject to the controller's tastes and ideas.

In addition, there is no system anywhere that is owned by Mexican-Americans and CTIC does not know of any potential franchises for which Mexican-Americans have bids. This is not too surprising in view of the fact that there are only three systems that are partially owned by blacks, and traditionally blacks have been ahead of Chicanos in media enterprises.[38]

One of the obvious problems facing minorities in the area of cable communication is the need for detailed and current information regarding the awarding of franchises and the legal provisions for the use of the public-access channels. However, good, solid information on this subject is not easily available at the community level, particularly to grassroots groups that are only vaguely aware of cable television's potential. Even when the information is thrust upon them, they often do not respond. This was the problem encountered by the organizers of the second Denver Media Conference in June 1972, when a cable workshop for minority activists was integrated into the conference. It was found that the cable workshop could not compete against workshops in the areas of radio, television, and newspaper, and that out of around 200 delegates, only a small handful were interested in cable. It soon became apparent that most of the delegates were so involved in trying to gain access to the established media that they had little time or desire to tackle the much more obscure objective of cablevision. Later that summer, at the First National Spanish-Speaking Radio Seminar in Washington, D.C., many delegates indicated that access to cable was too far off to satisfy their community requirements. They were interested primarily in immediate access to existing media and saw cable as being too distant to be of any importance.*

The question that must be asked here is this: If information is so vitally important to the public and to minority groups in particular, then who should be supplying this information? Barry Head, dealing with this question in the March 1973 issue of Harper's comes to the conclusion that the government should be the disseminator of such information, but is not fulfilling that function, and that private groups are not adequately staffed or funded to do the job quickly enough or thoroughly enough to do it well.

He charges that congressmen are uninformed, the FCC does not speak for the public interest, and the President's Office of Telecommunication Policy has no room in its job description for that role.[39] Furthermore, the Cable Television Information Center which is a semiautonomous unit within the Urban Institute, is of little help to the public groups that need on-the-site advocates, rather than just information, on request. A national group of interested individuals and agencies has formed Publi-Cable, Inc. as a voice of advocacy, but as Head sees it, "with no organization, no office, no money, and . . . no influence." One of the problems with the Publi-Cable group is that it is completely an ad hoc group whose 150 members, although well-connected with a variety of governmental and private agencies, all have full-time jobs to keep them busy and can therefore not deal with the multitude of problems at the local level.

The National Citizens Committee for Broadcasting, once active under the direction of Thomas Hoving in the area of public access, is

---

*The author attended both of these conferences and interviewed many of the delegates.

practically dormant and the United Church of Christ's Office of Communication, according to Head, is critically short of manpower and resources.[40] Albert Kramer's Citizens' Communication Center is too involved in license challenging to direct the cable effort and the newly-formed Cable Communication Resource Center in Washington, D.C. only went into operation in February 1973. As a minority cable consulting agency, it has worked on a very limited basis with Mexican-American groups. It is headed by black cable expert, Charles Tate, formerly of the Urban Institute. This has resulted in a situation in which the citizen is left to fend for himself in the area of cable communication, with the very distinct possibility that the potential of the medium for social action will go untapped for many years to come.

NOTES

1. Columbia Broadcasting System, Inc. v. Democratic National Committee, 41 U.S. Law Week 4688-4721.

2. Nicholas Johnson, remarks before the Minority Workshop on Cable Communication, Washington, D.C., June 24, 1971.

3. Charles Tate, Cable Television in the Cities (Washington, D.C.: The Urban Institute, 1971), p. 105.

4. "Countdown on Cable Television," Broadcasting, November 27, 1972, p. 51.

5. Tate, Cable Television, pp. 105-6.

6. Ibid., p. 105.

7. Kansas City Star, April 4, 1973.

8. Don Freeman, "FCC Lift of Freeze Raises Sights in San Diego," Variety, April 18, 1973, p. 40.

9. U.S. Department of Justice, Community Relations Service, "Guidelines for CRS Support and Field Specialists in Developing a CATV Project," Washington, D.C., pp. 1-4. Mimeographed and undated.

10. Tate, Cable Television, p. 3.

11. Office of Communication, United Church of Christ, A Short Course in Cable (New York: United Church of Christ, 1972), p. 3.

12. Ibid.

13. JCET News, August 1971, pp. 6-7.

14. Sloan Commission on Cable Communication, On the Cable (New York: McGraw-Hill, Inc., 1971), pp. 123-34.

15. JCET News, p. 6.

16. Ibid., p. 7.

17. Office of Communication, A Short Course, p. 9.

18. Ibid.

19. Ponchita Pierce, "On Cable: TV for the People, by the People," McCall's, August 1972, p. 33.

20. Ibid.

21. Ibid.

22. Anda Korsts, "Video Groups Plan," Chicago Journalism Review, March 1972, pp. 3-4.

23. Ibid.

24. Ibid., p. 4.

25. Ibid.

26. Ibid.

27. United States v. Midwest Video Corp. 441 F. 2d 1322 (8th cir. 1971).

28. John Rather and Christopher Burnett, "Local 'O' in San Francisco Gets an 'E' for Excellent," TV Communications, April 1973, p. 42.

29. "Public Access Sought on S.F. Cable System," Broadcasting, February 26, 1973, p. 61.

30. Barry Head, "Voices on the Cable," Harper's, March 1973, p. 32.

31. Ibid.

32. "Minorities Pact Clears Way for Merger of Cox, ATC," Broadcasting, December 4, 1972, p. 18.

33. "Countdown on Cable Television," p. 51.

34. Tom Edwards, supervisor of public utilities, city of San Antonio, telephone interview, May 21, 1972.

35. Gabrio Rodriquez, telephone interview, May 22, 1973.

36. David Green, program director of Bay Cablevision, Inc., Berkeley, Calif., telephone interview, May 22, 1973.

37. Mike Holland, telephone interview, May 22, 1973.

38. Ibid.

39. Head, "Voices on the Cable," p. 30.

40. Ibid., p. 32.

THE FUTURE AND
THE IMPLICATIONS
OF THE MOVEMENT

There are still many questions about the problems of media access and the civil rights of minorities that cannot be fully answered. For instance, can prejudice and racism actually be reduced or eliminated through manipulation of the mass media? Has the civil rights movement been successful in promoting understanding and compromise between minorities and media owners? Can the news media adapt to the cry for increased access without the need for increased government regulation? Where does the minority media movement stand, specifically the effort of Chicanos, in regard to their goals of media reform and involvement? Finally, will increased access to the media mean improved conditions for Mexican-Americans or any other minority group?

These are but a few of the unanswerable questions for which time alone will provide answers, but which should nevertheless be considered in light of the present indications. The following discussion will address itself to some of these questions and to the future of the Chicano Movement in communication.

TWO OPPOSING VIEWS

It is evident that today the media face an era of public distrust and misunderstanding, which, if carried to its furthest extremes, could promote a climite of opinion favorable toward more government regulation. For this reason it is vital that media owners understand the vocal minority of the American public who are clamoring for government-enforced access to the channels of communication. Indications that the media have generally failed to adapt to changing times are everywhere: the fantastic growth of the underground press; the rise of more than 20 critical journalism reviews; the broadcast challenge movement; attempts at local, state, and even national press councils; and a public outcry against irresponsible advertising. Yet, the great chasm between the media owner and the citizen activist still seems to exist and may continue to exist in spite of the recent success by minorities and citizen groups in forcing face-to-face confrontations.

Herman Kahn of the Hudson Institute believes that this chasm is caused by a serious division between classes in our society.[1] He speculates that an upper-middle class, made up of 20 percent of the population, expresses their views through the media that they control or influence. This makes the rest of society feel accused, neglected and, therefore, truculent. Just how truculent the lower classes feel toward the upper-class media owner is shown in a recent study conducted by the author. Under the auspices of the Freedom of Information Center, the author undertook a study in the spring of 1972 to determine the general attitudes of those involved in challenging the media in contrast to the attitudes of those who own and operate them.[2] The findings indicate that understanding is far from being reached.

Attitudes in the study were determined via Q-technique, a set of procedures developed by William Stephenson to study complex matters of human behavior—such as attitudes. Subjects operantly defined their attitudes by sorting 55 opinion statements concerning the media, according to their degree of agreement or disagreement. In Q, persons are factor analyzed across a sample of tests, resulting in clusters of persons (Q-factors) who have sorted the statements in similar, i.e., correlated ways. A Q-factor represents a hypothetical person—a kind of composite individual whose makeup is composed of all those individuals who are part of the factor.

The 40 subjects who participated in the study were selected on the basis of their backgrounds, with an effort to include persons with specific interests or involvement in the media. The object was to understand how those persons who are active in challenging the established press feel about the media as compared to how journalists feel. The resulting sample of people consisted of 40 persons categorized into five broad areas: print journalism, broadcast journalism, advertising, media challengers, and nonmedia. Included in the sample were newsmen, broadcasters, publishers, journalism students, journalism professors, editors of journalism reviews, nonjournalists involved in community radio stations, members of citizen pressure groups, minority members, consumer advocates, blue-collar workers and a few nonmedia professionals.[3]

Factor analysis resulted in a six-factor solution. In other words, the subjects fell into six major categories, or types, which the author interpreted and named. Of importance here are the two types that came up at opposite extremes. As could have been expected, those active in challenging the media, such as minority members (including Mexican-Americans) and citizen activists, all sorted the 55 statements in similar ways. This factor, or type of individual, was named "The Revolutionary," because of his desire for rapid social reform of the media. (It is significant to note that the attitude expressed in this factor was surprisingly prevalent among Chicano activists interviewed later by the author during the months of travel in which this work was researched. Literally dozens of people who had no knowledge of the study related opinions that were quite similar to those used in the Q sort.) At the opposite extreme was the "Staunch Defender," so named for his uncompromising and somewhat paranoid defense of the media. This factor was dominated by persons with extensive media experience, but with a predominance of people in broadcasting. Working broadcast journalists, newspaper publishers, and broadcast station owners and managers made up this factor.[4] A brief description of these two opposing types seems appropriate here, for they are symbolic of the two forces that have come to grips in the media movement.

The Revolutionary

This factor was defined by those involved in community broadcasting stations, those seeking access to the media, minority group members, editors of journalism reviews, and some journalists. Statements that typify this attitude tend to fall into three major categories: minority rights, corporate tyranny, and media irresponsibility. The most highly ranked statement was "Freedom of the press, as expressed in the First Amendment, means freedom for every citizen to have access to the nation's media." Such a statement is a radical departure from the traditional American belief that freedom of the press is basically the freedom of the media owner to print what he chooses without interference from government or any other outside source. Indeed, the other five types either disagreed strongly with this view or treated it as a neutral item.

The high ranking of this statement also indicates that there may be a significant portion of the population beginning to believe that the free press guarantee of the First Amendment does not solely apply to the press, but to the individual citizen as well.

The people on this factor place a high priority on the media's connection with big business and what they perceive as the powerful institutions that try to perpetuate the status quo. They agreed with the statement that the "establishment" media cannot serve the public "because they are organized to serve the advertiser"; "because class bias permeates the media, resulting in a distorted reflection of reality"; and "because rather than being an advocate for the underdog, the press is an advocate of nearly all the powerful institutions of the community.''

The Revolutionary views censorship in quite a different way from the traditional journalist:

A form of censorship already exists when the news is determined by a handful of men responsible only to their corporate employers and is filtered through a handful of commentators.

The emphasis on this type of statement implies that the Revolutionary is challenging the concept of ''laissez faire'' economics that he thinks has allowed big business to dominate the media. He believes that this is at least as great a threat to democracy and a free marketplace of ideas as government control of the media.

Statements rated negatively also illustrate this antagonism toward big business:

What is good for big business is good for the country.

If it were not for the advertising dollar, TV programming would be pathetic.

The end result of this pronounced antipathy toward the established press is a desire to provide a check-and-balance system to keep the media in line. Although direct censorship is completely ruled out—''No government agency should be set up to determine what is authentic or biased in news reporting.''—the Revolutionary believed that there must be government regulation—''Limited regulation of the media gives important minority views the right to be heard.'' The idea of nongovernmental advisory boards (press councils) to act as a conscience for the media did not strongly appeal to this type, although it was positively ranked.

Despite the low esteem in which they hold the media, persons on factor I are concerned about the rights of newsmen and the function of the press as an investigator of government affairs.

Generally speaking, the Revolutionary would like to see some drastic changes in the media and their role in society. He holds high the First Amendment guarantee of a free press, but would extend that guarantee to every citizen, not just to the owners of the media. In order to guarantee this right, he is willing to have some government control of the press, if it will ensure that minority views will be presented.[5]

152

The Staunch Defender

Statements that seemed to threaten the independence of the media or to infringe on their concept of First Amendment rights were ranked more negatively by the Staunch Defender than any other type.[6]

The two major areas of concern for the Staunch Defender are government interference with the media and pressures from special interest groups to gain access to the press.

The first two statements ranked most highly by this group read as if they had been edited into a paragraph:

No government agency should be set up to determine what is authentic or biased in news reporting.

Once the government gets its foot in the door even a little bit, government regulation of the media will grow. Eventually, we will have a press that is controlled by the government.

The pro-broadcast nature of this factor is also signified by the high value this group placed on this statement:

If First Amendment principles are held not to apply to the broadcast media, it may well be that the Constitution's guarantee of a free press is on its deathbed.

and by their extreme negative reaction to this one:

The history of broadcasting in the U.S. is littered with the bodies of those who wanted to do something significant and who were driven out by the pimps and thieves who now run the media.

Other highly-ranked statements tend to shed some light on how the Staunch Defender visualizes his role in the media. He defends the commercial nature of the media by saying that "If it were not for the advertising dollar, TV programming would be pathetic," and he admits that the media have a responsibility to "emphasize the good points of government policy." The Staunch Defender also ranked positively a statement that the Revolutionary would call a rationalization for the commercial nature of the media:

Broadcasting, as a mass commercial medium, has to give the majority of the people what they want, and what they want is entertainment and clever commercials.[7]

Several statements illustrate the degree to which broadcasters feel intimidated by criticism and by those seeking access. This type rated the two following statements more positively than any other:

Although there is nothing basically wrong with pressure groups conveying their ideas and recommendations to media, their tactics are often reprehensible.

The broadcasting system in the U.S. would be substantially destroyed or eroded if broadcasters were not provided with government protection against citizen pressure groups.

Statements with which this type disagreed more than any other also indicate a feeling of intimidation:

The press today seems paranoid. They call it free speech when they attack the government, but when government snaps back it's called intimidation.

I don't think the media have been hampered in their presentation of news by the government criticism.

The extreme reaction to many of these comments seems to show a strong feeling of resentment toward those who would encroach on the rights of the media to make autonomous judgments about what is to be presented. The Staunch Defender is less ready to criticize the media than are the other types and is more concerned with justifying the relationship between private enterprise and the mass media.[8]

The implications of this comparison of views are clear. Our social system is facing an era in which the traditional interpretation of press freedom is being challenged on the ground that media ownership (like the ownership of other businesses) is being concentrated in fewer and fewer hands, thereby systematically reducing a diversity of views. Also implied here is that the media owners and operators are not likely to relinquish their First Amendment freedoms voluntarily in favor of an enforced right of access imposed and regulated by the government. The question that still remains to be answered is whether the media movement will help close the chasm that exists between the "establishment" and the "disenfranchised," or whether the question of whom the First Amendment really refers to (the owner or the public) must be settled by the government.

THE MOVEMENT LOSES A FRIEND

Ironically, the federal government has been defending the media's independence with one hand (the Federal Communications Commission), while promoting public access with another (the Department of Justice's Community Relations Service). Meanwhile, the courts have walked the middle road, granting a limited right of access in areas such as license challenges, while protecting the sovereignty of the owner in his right to refuse controversial advertisements. This delicate balance within the government, however, has been tilted drastically in favor of the media recently, with the cutback of services to minorities from government agencies.

As the Community Relations Service's (CRS) communications section is dismantled, so too is much of the media movement's infrastructure and perhaps some of its grass-roots activities. For years the agency served as the only middleman between minorities and federal agencies, media representatives, and the various public-interest law groups. With its demise there will be no replacement. There is no other organization that can provide the national movement with the communication linkup or the mobility it needs to coordinate its efforts. What this will mean to the future of the Chicano Movement is difficult to estimate at this time, but much depends on the level of sophistication that its members have been able to achieve in the past few years. Attempts toward forming a substitute organization, such as the Chicano Media Council or a Chicano Media Information Center have not been successful and the possibility that the different law groups will join forces to direct the total effort seems remote.

At its peak in early 1973, the communications section had active communications programs in at least five major cities affecting Mexican-Americans and many others affecting other minority groups. Other programs were being developed even as the word came that all programs would have to be halted or transferred to other government agencies. According to CRS communications section chief Willis Selden, the effect on the communities involved is "discouraging for the future of the movement. This is due to the fact that no one else is prepared to take on the task."[9]

In order to understand the significance of the loss of CRS communications programs to the movement, it is imperative that they be outlined.

San Diego

In San Diego, CRS became involved in minority communications problems in 1969 during one of its crisis-response activities. The

155

agency assisted in the identification and securing of funds for an inter-racial television program and documentary publication titled "Sunday in the Park." This included the use of print and broadcast media in publicizing the public discussions which attempted to analyze what had happened to cause the crisis and how to avoid similar occurrences.[10] After this initial experience, CRS field representatives and regional support specialists met with principals of the Chicano Federation, the Southeast San Diego Communications Complex, Telemetas, and many other organizations to discuss communications problems. This dialogue led to the development of a CRS program (about to be imple-mented when CRS was cut back) centered around the Community News Center Council, a multiethnic community group whose chief concern is resolution of the black/brown communications problems. The council sought to establish a bilingual minority news center and asked CRS assistance in organizing and funding it.[11]

Chicago

Chicago's blacks and browns asked for and received aid from CRS with regard to the media in the form of a wide-ranging program that grew out of events that took place in 1970. In that year, CRS sponsored the Midwest Chicano Media Conference and helped in the formation of the Chicago Broadcast Coalition which was organized to deal with programming and personnel problems in the electronic media.[12] The latter effort resulted in several license challenges by the Coalition, which in turn led to a series of negotiations and an ulti-mate agreement between the Coalition and ABC and CBS outlets.

The CRS's communications program for Chicago was centered around the five-point agreement that included minority employment and training, community participation in broadcast advertising prac-tices, minority economic development, and programming.[13] The pro-gram was based on assisting the minority groups in Chicago in imple-menting the agreements and in seeking additional such agreements with all other broadcast outlets in the area. Other program activities included aid to minority organizations seeking CATV franchises and access, at a time when the city government was deciding the future of cable television. Also, CRS was active in establishing a media training program for minorities at Malcolm X College and other Chicago area educational institutions.[14]

San Francisco

The San Francisco-Oakland area began receiving CRS media assistance in February 1969, when residents of the Hunters Point

Model Neighborhood requested assistance in developing a low-watt television station that would be community owned and operated.[15] The station's purpose was to serve both as a communications medium for the area and as a training ground for minority youths in broadcasting. Efforts to raise funds for this project proved fruitless, and with CRS help, the concept was altered to aim for a CATV channel or a UHF station. The Model Cities program earmarked $714,000 to support the project as a result. In November of the following year, CRS staff and consultants helped bring together a multiracial coalition called the Bay Area Committee for Media Change, which eventually was responsible for the negotiation of several important agreements with broadcasters.

A continuing six-point communications program was developed by CRS, centered around the Coalition and the implementation of the agreements in that area:

1. Work with them to establish objectives as they see the needs.

2. Provide technical assistance to them related to the fundamentals in programming and employment policy and practice.

3. Assist in generating interest in broadcast media among high school and college students to assist in monitoring stations.

4. Assist in the establishment of a communications skills workshop within the Coalition for community leaders interested in working in the local media project to increase their sophistication in media operations.

5. Assist in the formulation of the agreements to be negotiated for each individual station.

6. Encourage in-house training opportunities for upward mobility of present employees.[16]

Four other areas were outlined as possible future activities of the Bay Area communications program, which, when completed, would have helped insure the influence of minorities in the media:

1. Contacting colleges and universities in the Bay Area and encouraging them to specialize in programs which will give minorities training in broadcasting.

2. Out of the Coalition, establish a community media committee to be an ongoing umbrella organization for initiating and sponsoring various activities to assure achievement of its objectives.

3. Assist in the establishment of work-study media programs, summer programs modeled after the Columbia University program, and part-time programs geared to those in the minorities who are interested in careers in broadcasting and who could acquire the needed specifics to move into broadcasting with a few months' training.

4. Assist the minority community in negotiating for increased union membership, the better to assure the possibilities for equal opportunity in employment.[17]

Los Angeles

CRS communication specialists evaluated the Los Angeles situation this way:

The communications field in Los Angeles . . . is dominated by the majority's system of values. This means that the voice of the minority community is not heard and the daily life of the minority community is not seen. . . . Prior to the (1965 riots), mass media conspicuously discriminated against blacks, browns, and other minorities through employment, slanted news coverage, and cultural bias.[18]

To help minorities combat these problems, CRS began meeting with minority organizations such as Nosotros, IMAGE, Justicia, and others in an effort to develop a long-range program. Finally, in February 1972, the CRS communications program for Los Angeles was officially approved. It focused on three specific areas: media recruitment, training, and ethnic communication centers. In order to help solve the problems of recruitment and training, CRS began assisting in the formation of a coalition steering committee composed of media activists, minority media employees, media executives, educators, and union leaders. The function of the committee was to develop studies, programs, and specific guidelines for increasing minority career opportunities in the industry.[19]

The purpose of the ethnic communication centers is threefold: (1) to provide a vehicle for intergroup communications, (2) to provide a place for different ethnic and racial groups to learn to use various communication techniques to deal with social problems, and (3) to provide a pool of information for identifying and developing talent in the minority community.[20]

San Bernardino and Fresno

Two other programs that will either be discontinued or shifted to other agencies exist in San Bernardino and Fresno, California. In San Bernardino, CRS was asked to assist Chicano and black media activists in developing broadcast participation with a local educational television station. The management of the station, KVCR-TV at San Bernardino Valley College, also requested assistance for the specific purpose of establishing rapport with minority groups interested in communication.[21] A communication program was structured by CRS around these requests, with the agency committing itself to provide technical and logistical assistance.

In Fresno, a program was designed to assist in the implementation of the Capital Cities Broadcasting agreement which pledged $88,300 per year for three years to minority groups in that city. The money is being used for training and programming in minority interests and requires considerable expertise. The Minority Advisory Committee (MAC) serves as the official organization under which the agreement is to be implemented and is composed of twenty minority members—eight black, twelve brown—and the general manager of the station (KFSN-TV).[22] Goals of the CRS program are to help the MAC expand its scope and influence in Fresno to other TV and radio stations, to render technical assistance in order to insure that moneys allocated are spent in programming that reflects the values of the minority communities, and to assist the MAC and the station in the development of a training program that will result in increased minority employment in telecommunications.[23]

Selden was concerned with the future of the movement as a result of CRS cutbacks. When the section closed its activities on June 30, 1973, programmatic activity in communication by the federal government for the most part came to a halt. "There just isn't any federal or private organization that is set up to take over our projects," Selden explained. "Our function as a loose communication network for minority groups active in media projects will not be taken up by another organization."[24]

Selden mentioned a few agencies that might be able to carry on some of the work in the areas of funding and technical assistance. Some of these are the White House's Cabinet Committee on Opportunity for the Spanish Speaking; FCC Commissioner Benjamin Hook's new proposed minorities affairs section; the United Church of Christ; the United Presbyterian Church; and the United Methodist Church, which is now funding some Chicano media groups. The Office of Economic Opportunity (OEO) was intending to become involved in this type of activity, but it was also disbanded under the Nixon administration. It was rumored in Washington that FCC Commissioner Nicholas

Johnson might establish an organization to act as a national center for the assistance of citizen groups who are challenging broadcast licenses or who have already signed agreements and are having difficulties implementing them. However, Johnson stated flatly in early April 1973 (two months before his term as commissioner expired) that this would not be the case. "There is definitely a need for such an organization, but I am not in a position to organize such an effort. There would be great funding problems to overcome."[25]

Thus, there is some question of how the media activities of the Chicano Movement will fare in the future, without the help of a friend.

WHERE THE MOVEMENT STANDS

Prospects for media access for the Chicano Movement would seem brighter if the movement would begin to address itself to the vital area of cable television. Its lack of knowledge and effort in this area may prove to be its greatest failure. Equally to blame is the federal government for not providing the vehicle through which the public can be thoroughly informed about this complex subject. This lack of effort, together with the curtailment of the work done by the Community Relations Service, is a great threat to the progress of the movement.

But even with a concentrated effort, the time is not yet here when the technology will allow massive doses of minority programming. For the next few years, emphasis will remain on consuming the trickle of air time that years of legal fighting have dislodged from the controllers of the media. In fact, it appears that the fight for commercial air time will continue right up to the time when a community group wins what appears to be a significant battle, only to turn around and be handed an entire channel to program. As that time approaches, there is an increasing need for skilled and experienced program producers and technicians who will be able to fill the time with worthwhile programming.

Indeed, the long-range problem seems to be one of logistics rather than of strategy. Where will the money come from to produce the programming to fill the public-access, educational, and local-origination channels of the near future? Once there are unlimited channels, and air time becomes cheap as dirt for the average American, where will the manpower come from to ensure that the channels do not remain empty?

Already there is an indication that public-access channels will go unused. In New York and Berkeley, the program directors for the first public-access channels have found it difficult to get material for airing. Managers of commercial stations, who are responsible for seeing that minority agreements are fulfilled, are finding that the challenging groups are having a hard time producing the programming after the contract is signed. All in all, it appears that the movement is on the brink of a new technological era that will revolutionize communication in society. In this respect, we are all grossly ill-prepared for what lies ahead. People are not geared, nor are they accustomed, to using electronic communication to the extent that will be necessary ten years from now. The first effects of this new freedom of communication is evident in our society's ignorance of the skills needed in the use of film and video tape.

But what of the efforts of the movement in the past few years? Has anything been accomplished? It is difficult, perhaps impossible, to measure the gains made by the Chicano Movement in the area of communication since the marches of the grape pickers. However, certain generalizations can be made safely. First, there has been a significant gain in the area of programming at the local level as a result of the broadcast challenges and the subsequent agreements. Every agreement has resulted in new public-affairs programs for Chicanos and has put pressure on other stations to do the same. As a result, Chicano groups at the local level throughout the Southwest have programs, like "Perspectiva" and "Noticias" in El Paso, through which they communicate their problems, albeit at nine o'clock on Sunday morning.

In addition, the print media at the local level have begun to respond, ever so slowly, by attempting to give more coverage to their Mexican-American constituencies. One example is the San Antonio News, which established a weekly, bilingual tabloid called The Sun. The tabloid averages 24 pages of news and features pertaining to Mexican-Americans and is distributed to its 63,786 subscribers every Thursday with the parent paper.[26]

Another indication of some progress is the increased foundation and government interest in funding minority programming. An example of this type of assistance is the approval of a $3.5 million grant in July 1973 from the U.S. Office of Education to a bilingual children's television venture aimed at reducing educational handicaps among minority group youngsters.[27] The material, ranging from spot announcements for a national audience to a full series, will be primarily for elementary and secondary school-age viewers. The grant to Bicultural Children's Television, Inc., of Oakland, California, will finance the production of 65 half-hour bilingual children's programs for use by Public Broadcasting Service stations.

The movement has also made the national media aware of the issues of racism, ethnic identity, poor living conditions, and law enforcement injustice. One who has seen these changes taking place for many years is actor Henry Darrow, who changed his name from

Henry Delgado to escape the Latin stereotype. Today, he is still being cast in that role, but enjoys playing a Mexican-American detective in a TV series called "Hernandez." In 1969, he helped Ricardo Montalban organize Nosotros, an organization established to improve the image of Spanish-speaking people within the entertainment industry.28 Darrow believes that the movement has been fairly successful "not only in front of the cameras, but in the arts and crafts. The thing I see is the young performers with talent getting breaks earlier than I did. . . . That has to be an indication of progress. There is an awareness within the industry."

This new awareness is already having a subtle impact on society. There are more brown faces on the television screens today as a result of the movement and who can measure the effect that fact alone will have on the new generation of Mexican-Americans who are reminded daily that opportunity is not only a word for Anglo children?

All of this indicates that there have been significant inroads made by the Chicano Movement in incorporating the mass media into their culture, yet the progress has been difficult and laborious because of its disorganization and lack of leadership. Are the media efforts more organized now, after years of struggle? With the demise of CRS and the failure of the movement to establish a national coordinating center, the answer to this question must be a definite "no." Organization is one of the areas in which the movement is most lacking, even if only for the sake of transmission of crucial information that is so necessary at the community level. There seems to be little hope that any form of loose coordination on a national scale can succeed, thus forcing local media groups to rely on Anglo or black groups for information and advice. However, it isn't likely that this lack of organization will cause the movement to stop its progress. There is much too much work to be done to implement the victories that have been won. The course has been set for more minority involvement in the media at every level and it is just a matter of time until the educational system will produce a significantly larger number of well-trained and highly qualified minority people to enter the field of communication. The greatest effect that the lack of national organization will have on the movement, it now appears, is in delaying its progress.

Finally, it must be asked if the media movement has helped to relieve the tension in the barrios to the extent that riots are not likely to be the format of social protest in the future. As the movement stands prior to an era of increased access, the answer to this question also has to be "no." There is not yet enough emphasis or recognition of Mexican-American problems in the media. Riots are caused by frustration that evolves from a feeling that no one, not even the government, cares about the problems of the barrio. It takes more than a few half-hour segments at 9 o'clock on Sunday morning or an occasional column in the Sunday paper to alleviate this problem. It takes concentrated coverage and in-depth reporting to provide the type of relief that is necessary to prevent this kind of violence. And it is the challenge of the media to provide this service, even after the era of public access has arrived.

NOTES

1. Christian Science Monitor, July 7, 1973.
2. Joe Lewels, Jr., "Critical Attitudes toward the Media," Freedom of Information Center Report No. 281, May 1972, p. 1.
3. Ibid., p. 2.
4. Ibid.
5. Ibid.
6. Ibid., p. 5.
7. Ibid., p. 6.
8. Ibid.
9. Willis Selden, telephone interview, April 2, 1973.
10. U.S. Department of Justice, Community Relations Service, "Communications Program for the City of San Diego, California," Washington, D.C., February 17, 1972, pp. 1-10. Mimeographed.
11. Ibid., p. 7.
12. U.S. Department of Justice, Community Relations Service, "Communications Program for the City of Chicago, Illinois," Washington, D.C., February 10, 1972, p. 1. Mimeographed.
13. Ibid., Appendix B.
14. Ibid., p. 6.
15. U.S. Department of Justice, Community Relations Service, "Communications Program for the Cities of San Francisco and Oakland, California," Washington, D.C., August 10, 1971, pp. 1-17. Mimeographed.
16. Ibid., p. 10.
17. Ibid., pp. 10-11.
18. U.S. Department of Justice, Community Relations Service, "Communications Program for the City of Los Angeles," Washington, D.C., February 10, 1972, p. 1. Mimeographed.
19. Ibid., p. 11.
20. Ibid., p. 12.
21. U.S. Department of Justice, Community Relations Service, "Communications Program for the City of San Bernardino, California," Washington, D.C., April 17, 1972, p. 1. Mimeographed.
22. U.S. Department of Justice, Community Relations Service, Communications Program for the City of Fresno, California," Washington, D.C., May 9, 1972, p. 5. Mimeographed.

23. Ibid., pp. 8-9.
24. Selden, telephone interview, April 2, 1973.
25. Nicholas Johnson, telephone interview, April 2, 1973.
26. Mike Esparza, "The Chicano Press," Arizona Journalist, Fall 1971, p. 6.
27. Washington Post, July 3, 1973.
28. El Paso Times, January 15, 1973.

SPANISH-SURNAME POPULATION FIGURES

State	Number of Spanish-Surname People	Percentage of Total Population
Alabama	13,313	—
Alaska	6,279	2
Arizona	333,349	19
Arkansas	9,333	—
California	3,101,589	16
Colorado	286,467	13
Connecticut	73,357	2
Delaware	6,267	1
District of Columbia	15,671	2
Florida	451,382	7
Georgia	29,824	1
Hawaii	23,267	3
Idaho	18,476	3
Illinois	364,397	3
Indiana	67,188	1
Iowa	17,448	1
Kansas	46,706	2
Kentucky	11,112	—
Louisiana	69,678	2
Maine	3,730	—
Maryland	52,974	1
Massachusetts	64,860	1
Michigan	120,687	1
Minnesota	23,198	1
Mississippi	8,182	—
Missouri	40,640	1
Montana	7,771	1
Nebraska	21,067	1
Nevada	27,142	6
New Hampshire	2,681	—
New Jersey	135,678	2
New Mexico	407,286	40
New York	872,471	5
North Carolina	22,611	—
North Dakota	2,007	—
Ohio	95,128	1
Oklahoma	36,007	1
Oregon	34,577	2
Pennsylvania	44,535	—
Rhode Island	6,961	1
South Carolina	10,999	—
South Dakota	2,954	—
Tennessee	13,873	—
Texas	2,059,671	18
Utah	43,550	4
Vermont	2,469	1
Virginia	48,742	1
Washington	70,734	2
West Virginia	6,261	—
Wisconsin	41,402	1
Wyoming	18,551	6

Source: These statistics were compiled by the U.S. Census Bureau and are available in more detail from the U.S. Government Printing Office in publication P.C. 1 (1)-C General Social and Economic Characteristics of the United States, 1972.

MINORITIES IN COMMERCIAL TELEVISION, NATIONWIDE AND BY STATE

	Total	Black	Percent	Spanish Surnames	Percent	Officials and Managers	Professionals
NATIONWIDE							
Full time 1972	39,071	2,644	6.8	1,048	2.7	127	207
Full time 1971	38,619	2,280	5.9	858	2.2	115	159
Part time 1972	3,811	488	12.8	161	4.2	0	34
Part time 1971	3,738	430	11.5	128	3.4	2	27
						White Collar Production	
Trainees 1972	781	162	20.7	171	21.9	77	94
Trainees 1971	766	161	21.0	27	3.5	18	9
TEXAS							
Full time 1972	2,704	126	4.7	223	8.2	21	31
Full time 1971	2,671	100	3.7	203	7.6	20	28
Part time 1972	260	28	10.8	34	13.1	—	7
Part time 1971	285	21	7.4	26	9.1	—	3
						White Collar Production	
Trainees 1972	82	5	6.1	13	5.8	9	4
Trainees 1971	70	3	4.3	7	10.0	5	2
CALIFORNIA							
Full time 1972	3,734	213	5.7	250	6.7	25	61
Full time 1971	3,655	173	4.7	183	5.0	11	37
Part time 1972	284	26	9.1	29	10.2	—	7
Part time 1971	258	21	8.1	18	6.9	—	7
						White Collar Production	
Trainees 1972	29	9	10.3	9	10.3	7	2
Trainees 1971	52	7	13.5	8	15.4	7	1

	Total	Black	Percent	Spanish Surnames	Percent	Officials and Managers	Professionals
ARIZONA							
Full time 1972	598	23	3.8	40	6.7	4	5
Full time 1971	580	23	3.9	26	4.9	1	3
Part time 1972	87	5	5.7	8	9.1	—	—
Part time 1971	76	7	9.2	7	9.2	—	—
						White Collar Production	
Trainees 1972	2	1	50.0	—	—	—	—
Trainees 1971	4	2	50.0	1	25.0	—	1
COLORADO							
Full time 1972	540	16	3.0	26	4.9	1	6
Full time 1971	528	15	2.8	19	3.6	1	2
Part time 1972	61	3	4.9	3	4.9	—	—
Part time 1971	56	5	8.9	5	8.9	—	1
						White Collar Production	
Trainees 1972	1	—	—	—	—	—	—
Trainees 1971	1	1	100.0	—	—	—	—
NEW MEXICO							
Full time 1972	202	1	.5	16	7.9	2	3
Full time 1971	203	—	—	13	6.4	—	1
Part time 1972	45	4	8.9	15	33.0	—	1
Part time 1971	37	—	—	8	21.6	—	1
						White Collar Production	
Trainees 1972	7	—	—	1	14.2	1	0
Trainees 1971	—	—	—	—	—	—	—

Source: The data herewith were extracted from the computer printout used by the United Church of Christ in a study on minority hiring in 1972. Their information was obtained from the Federal Communication Commission's equal employment opportunity forms, which each station is required to complete.

BOOKS

Allport, Gordon. The Nature of Prejudice. Cambridge, Mass.: Addison-Wesley, 1954.

Blumer, Herbert. "Social Movements." In Studies in Social Movements, edited by Barry McLaughlin. New York: The Free Press, 1969.

Briegel, Kaye. "The Development of Mexican-American Organizations." In The Mexican-Americans: An Awakening Minority, edited by Manuel Servin. Beverly Hills, Calif.: Glencoe Press, 1970.

Burma, John H. Spanish-Speaking Groups in the United States. Durham, N.C.: Duke University Press, 1954.

Carranza, Eliu. On Los Chicanos: A Cultural Revolution. Berkeley, Calif.: California Book Co., 1969.

Casavantes, Edward J. A New Look at the Attributes of the Mexican-American. Albuquerque, N. Mex.: Southwestern Cooperative Education Laboratory Inc., 1969.

Day, Mark. Forty Acres. New York: Praeger Publishers, 1971.

Duane, Frank. "A People and a Program." In Broadcasting and Social Action—A Handbook for Station Executives. Washington, D.C.: National Association of Broadcasters, November 1969.

Dunne, John Gregory. Delano. New York: Farrar, Straus and Giroux, 1967.

Gonzales, Rodolfo (Corky). "Chicano Nationalism: The Key to Unity for La Raza." In A Documentary History of the Mexican-American, edited by Wayne Moguin. New York: Praeger Publishers, 1971.

Guzman, Ralph. "The Gentle Revolutionaries." In Selected Reading Materials on the Mexican and Spanish American. Denver: Commission on Community Relations, City and County of Denver, April 1971.

Heller, Celia S. Mexican-American Youth. New York: Random House, 1966.

Hernandez, Luis F. A Forgotten American. New York: Anti-Defamation League of B'nai B'rith, 1969.

Hocking, William Ernest. Freedom of the Press. Chicago: University of Chicago Press, 1947.

Johnson, Nicholas. How to Talk Back to Your Television Set. Boston: Little, Brown & Co., 1969.

Lippman, Walter. Public Opinion. New York: Harcourt, Brace & Co., 1922.

McDonagh, Edward, and Richards, Eugene S. Ethnic Relations in the U.S. New York: Appleton, 1953.

Macias, Ysidro Ramon. "The Chicano Movement." In A Documentary History of the Mexican-American, edited by Wayne Moguin. New York: Praeger Publishers, 1971.

Madsen, William. The Mexican Americans of South Texas. New York: Holt, Rinehart, and Winston, 1964.

Moreno, Edward. "The Spanish Language Market: Promises, Premises, and Possibilities." In Broadcasting and Social Action— A Handbook for Station Executives. Washington, D.C.: National Association of Broadcasters, November 1969.

Nabokov, Peter. Tijerina and the Courthouse Raid. Albuquerque, N. Mex.; University of New Mexico Press, 1969.

National Advisory Commission on Civil Disorders (Kerner Commission). Report of the National Advisory Commission on Civil Disorders. New York: Bantam Books, Inc., 1968.

Nelson, Eugene. Huelga: The First Hundred Days of the Great Delano Grape Strike. Delano: Farm Worker Press, 1966.

Niven, Harold, ed. Broadcasting and Social Action—A Handbook for Station Executives. Washington, D.C.: National Association of Broadcasters, November 1969.

_____. Colleges and Universities with Minority Group Students Studying Broadcasting. Washington, D.C.: National Association of Broadcasters, 1972.

Office of Communication, United Church of Christ. A Short Course in Cable. New York: United Church of Christ, June 1972.

Pitt, Leonard. The Decline of the Californios. Berkeley, Calif.: University of California Press, 1970.

Rendon, Armando. The Chicano Manifesto. New York: Macmillan Co., 1971.

Rodriquez, Armando M. "Who Is La Raza?" In A Documentary History of the Mexican-Americans, edited by Wayne Moguin. New York: Praeger Publishers, 1971.

Sanchez, George. "The American of Mexican Descent." In Selected Reading Materials on the Mexican and Spanish Americans, edited by Maurice Velasquez. Denver: Commission on Community Relations, City and County of Denver, April 1971.

Servin, Manuel, ed. The Mexican-Americans: An Awakening Minority. Beverly Hills, Calif.: Glencoe Press, 1970.

Simmons, Ozzie G. "The Mutual Images and Expectations of Anglo-Americans and Mexican-Americans." In Mexican-Americans in the United States, edited by John H. Burma. Cambridge, Mass.: Canfield Press, 1970.

Sloan Commission on Cable Communication. On the Cable. New York: McGraw Hill, Inc., 1971.

Tate, Charles. Cabletelevision in the Cities. Washington, D.C.: The Urban Institute, 1971.

Tebbel, John. The Compact History of the American Newspaper. New York: Hawthorn Books, Inc., 1969.

Tuck, Ruth D. Not with the Fist. New York: Harcourt, Brace & Co., 1946.

Valdez, Daniel, and Pino, Tom. Ethnic Labels in Majority-Minority Relations. Denver: La Luz Publications, 1971.

MAGAZINE AND JOURNAL ARTICLES

"A Rift in the Challenger's Ranks." Broadcasting, October 4, 1971, pp. 26-27.

"Americans in the Mid West." Chicago Magazine, Autumn 1969, pp. 83-86.

"Anti-Defamation Group Fights Ads Using Spanish Name Stereotypes." Advertising Age, September 30, 1968, p. 94.

"Any Real Progress in Border Dispute with Tijuana FM's?" Broadcasting, August 14, 1972, p. 45.

Atkins, Jeanni. "Chicano Media Challenge: Basta Ya!" Freedom of Information Center Report No. 282, May 1972, pp. 1-7.

Bennet, Joseph. "They Used to Say 'It's Impossible, Baby.'" TV Guide, April 24, 1971, pp. 6-12.

Bongartz, Roy. "The Chicano Rebellion." The Nation, March 3, 1969, pp. 271-73.

"Burch's Charge to Cable Systems." Broadcasting, May 22, 1972, p. 24.

Burges, Toby. "Poll of Mexican-Americans." Arizona Journalist, Fall 1971, pp. 4-8.

"Cable Access." Broadcasting, December 11, 1972, p. 66.

Carpio, Salvadore. "Commission Report on Mexican-American Education—What It Means." La Luz, May 1972, pp. 9-10.

Carson, Donald W. "Jobs." Arizona Journalist, Fall 1971, pp. 4-5.

Casavantes, Edward. "Pride and Prejudice: A Mexican-American Dilemma." Civil Rights Digest, Winter 1970, pp. 22-27.

"Catchword in California Renewals: Minorities." Broadcasting, November 8, 1971, pp. 42-43.

171

"Challenged Stations Speak Out on Coast." Broadcasting, November 29, 1971, p. 61.

"Challengers Seek Station Figures." Broadcasting, July 26, 1971, pp. 21-22.

"Charges Untrue, WOAI-TV Answers." Broadcasting, September 6, 1971, p. 32.

"Chicano." Arizona Journalist, Fall 1971, p. 5.

"Chicanos Plan Organization." Broadcasting, August 14, 1972, p. 42.

"Chicanos' Question: What about Us?" Broadcasting, June 28, 1971, p. 23.

"Closed Circuit." Broadcasting, August 30, 1971, p. 7.

"Countdown on Cable Television." Broadcasting, November 27, 1972, p. 51.

"Cox-American Deal with Minorities Draws Fire at FCC." Broadcasting, December 18, 1972, pp. 48-49.

del Olmo, Frank. "Voices for the Chicano Movement." The Quill, October 1971, pp. 9-11.

"Diverse Appeals to D.C. Court." Broadcasting, July 3, 1972, p. 12.

"Doubleday and Chicanos Get Less Than Nowhere." Broadcasting, August 30, 1971, p. 8.

Drummond, William J. "The Death of a Man in the Middle." Esquire, April 1972, pp. 75-78.

Dugger, Ronnie. "Ballot-Box Revolution: The Political Awakening of Mexican-Americans in Texas." Frontier, September 1963, pp. 7-9.

"Editorials." Broadcasting, November 8, 1971, p. 66.

"8 Challenged Stations Win Renewals from FCC." Broadcasting, January 1, 1973, p. 6.

"Enter the Alianza in Renewal Attacks." Broadcasting, August 23, 1971, pp. 34-35.

Esparza, Mike. "The Chicano Press." Arizona Journalist, Fall 1971, p. 6.

"Ethnic Dispute in San Antonio." Broadcasting, July 5, 1971, p. 28.

"FCC Chairman Outlines New Commission Rulings." JCET News, August 1971, pp. 1-7.

"FCC Rejects Challenges in San Antonio, Buffalo." Broadcasting, November 27, 1972, pp. 8-9.

"FCC Won't Open Books of Albuquerque TVs." Broadcasting, September 6, 1971, p. 33.

"Federal Agency Rulings." Law Week, September 14, 1971, p. 2133.

"Firm Gets Contract for Spanish Programing." CATV, June 26, 1972, p. 12.

"First Chicano Press." Somos Aztlan, January 1970, p. 13.

Freeman, Don. "FCC Lift of Freeze Raises Sights of 18 Cable Systems in San Diego." Variety, April 18, 1973, p. 40.

"FTC is Working with Chicago Spanish-Speaking." Broadcasting, April 1972, pp. 1 + 4.

Galvez, Joe. "A Young Journalist Speaks/Activism and the Downtown Dailies." Arizona Journalist, Fall 1971, p. 3.

"Hard Bargains for KQEO Too." Broadcasting, November 29, 1971, pp. 58-59.

Head, Barry. "Voices on the Cable." Harper's, March 1973, pp. 30-33.

"Here Come the Challengers Again." Broadcasting, July 19, 1971, pp. 58-59.

"Hispanos Grossly Under-Represented in Federal Jobs." La Luz, May 1972, pp. 50-51.

"How Much Public Access Can Cable Really Stand?" Broadcasting, May 22, 1972, p. 10.

"Inch by Inch, FCC Moves Ahead on Renewal Cases." Broadcasting, November 13, 1972, p. 25.

Johnson, Nicholas. "The American Dream—Can the Private Good Work Also to the Best Public Good?" CATV, May 15, 1972, p. 25.

_____. "The Easy Chair." Harper's, February 1969, pp. 44-45.

Kaufman, Dave. "U.S. Equal Opportunity Commission Puts Network TV Coast Execs on Hot Seat Re Jobs for Minorities." Variety, March 19, 1969, p. 26.

_____. "2-Mil. Mexicans Can't Be Conned, Says Martel; Also-Angry Negro Actors Copping Latin Roles." Variety, September 25, 1968, p. 52.

"KEST Strikes Bargain with Citizen Groups." Broadcasting, March 13, 1972, p. 16.

Korsts, Anda. "Video Groups Plan." Chicago Journalism Review, March 1972, pp. 3-4.

Levine, Frank. "Spanish-Lingo Broadcasting Booms, with Visions of a 'Fourth Network' but Bargains Still to Be Hurdled." Variety, August 9, 1972, pp. 35 + 47.

Lewels, Joe, Jr. "Critical Attitudes toward the Media." Freedom of Information Center Report No. 281, May 1972, pp. 1-7.

_____. "Expansion of the Fairness Doctrine." Freedom of Information Center Report No. 251, November 1970, pp. 1-4.

_____. "The Newspaper Preservation Act." Freedom of Information Center Report No. 254, January 1971, pp. 1-5.

Loveland, David C. "Citizen Groups Challenge Radio-TV." Freedom of Information Center Report No. 256, February 1971, pp. 1-5.

"McGraw-Hill Sets Record for Concessions to Minorities." Broadcasting, May 15, 1972, pp. 25-26.

Martinez, Thomas. "How Advertisers Promote Racism." Civil Rights Digest, Fall 1969, pp. 5-11.

Matthiessen, Peter. "Profiles, Organizer P.I." The New Yorker, June 21, 1969, pp. 42-62.

_____. "Profiles, Organizer P. II." The New Yorker, June 28, 1969, pp. 42-63.

"Media Briefs." Broadcasting, November 27, 1972, p. 38.

"Metromedia Tries to Block Financial-Disclosure Ruling." Broadcasting, December 11, 1972, p. 31.

"Mexicans' Defenders Err." Advertising Age, March 16, 1970, p. 20.

"Minorities Gang Up in Albuquerque." Broadcasting, September 6, 1971, p. 33.

"Minorities Pact Clears Way for Merger of Cox, ATC." Broadcasting, December 4, 1972, pp. 18-19.

"Minority Group Loses in Denver." Broadcasting, August 9, 1971, p. 20.

Montez, Philip. "Will the Real Mexican-American Please Stand Up?" Civil Rights Digest, Winter 1970, pp. 28-31.

"NAB Presses Drive for Renewal Relief." Broadcasting, December 4, 1972, p. 38.

"NBC Answers Chicano Beefs on Portrayals." Variety, August 4, 1971, p. 2.

"NCTA Panels Provide Forum for Varied Views on Cable." Broadcasting, May 22, 1972, p. 13.

"Newest Guardians of Public Interest." Broadcasting, July 12, 1971, p. 37.

"Open Season on Texas Stations." Broadcasting, August 9, 1971, pp. 19-20.

Pierce, Ponchita. "On Cable: TV for the People, by the People." McCall's, August 1972, p. 33.

"Public Access Sought on S. F. Cable System." Broadcasting, February 26, 1973, p. 61.

Rather, John, and Burnett, Christopher. "Local 'O' in San Francisco Gets an 'E' for Excellent." TV Communications, April 1973, pp. 57-58.

Rendon, Armando. "La Raza—Today, Not Manana." Civil Rights Digest, Spring 1968, pp. 7-17.

"Renewal Battles in the Rockies." Broadcasting, March 8, 1971, p. 32.

Roth, Morry. "Growing Awareness of Minority Rights Cues License Challenges." Variety, March 31, 1971, p. 32.

Roybal, Edward R. "Federal Caste System against the Spanish-Speaking." Congressional Record, March 30, 1972, pp. 142-43.

"San Antonio Coalition Asks FCC to Revoke Licenses of 3 Outlets." Variety, July 7, 1971, p. 26.

"Scene of Crime." Broadcasting, November 8, 1971, p. 66.

"Senate Bill Appears for Renewal Protection." Broadcasting, October 4, 1971, p. 6.

Shaw, Bernard. "The Second Largest Minority: A News Correspondent's View." Civil Rights Digest, Fall 1970, pp. 9-12.

Shayon, Robert Lewis. "TV-Radio." Saturday Review, May 15, 1971, p. 54.

_____. "TV-Radio." Saturday Review, October 16, 1971, p. 73.

"Signs of Changing Times in Renewals." Broadcasting, May 17, 1971, pp. 34-35.

"6 Chicanos File Complaint with FCC Re KVOU 'Unresponsiveness' to Needs." Variety, October 7, 1970, p. 24.

Skrabenek, R. L. "Language Maintenance among Mexican-Americans." Civil Rights Digest, Spring 1971, pp. 18-24.

"Spanish Market: Undersold, Undervalued." Broadcasting, September 19, 1966, pp. 67-70.

Steiner, Stan. "Militance among the Mexican-Americans." The New
    Republic, June 20, 1970, pp. 16-18.

Tebbel, John. "Newest TV Boom: Spanish-Language Stations."
    Saturday Review, June 8, 1968, pp. 70-72.

"The Chicanos Campaign for a Better Deal." Business Week, May
    29, 1971, pp. 48-54.

"The Dust Hasn't Settled after Speech by Whitehead." Broadcasting,
    January 1, 1973, pp. 18-20.

"The Little Strike That Grew to La Causa." Time, July 4, 1969, pp.
    16-21.

"Time's $69-Million Sale Clears FCC." Broadcasting, March 13,
    1972, p. 20.

"Tio Taco Is Dead." Newsweek, June 29, 1970, pp. 22-28.

Toy, Steve. "U.S. Solons Ask Firm Stand on Border Beams in Treaty
    with Mex." Variety, August 2, 1972, p. 22.

"U.S. Latins on the March." Newsweek, May 23, 1966, pp. 32-35.

Weeks, Douglas. "The League of United Latin American Citizens:
    A Texas-Mexican Civic Organization." Southwestern Political
    and Social Science Quarterly, X (December 1929), pp. 257-78.

"Whitehead Bill Joins the Crowd Seeking to Ease Renewal Trauma."
    Broadcasting, January 1, 1973, pp. 24-25.

Zeidenberg, Leonard. "The Struggle over Broadcast Access." Broad-
    casting, September 20, 1971, pp. 32-41.

SPECIAL DOCUMENTS

Cabinet Committee on Opportunities for Spanish-Speaking People.
    A New Era. Washington, D.C.: U.S. Government Printing
    Office, Fall 1970.

U.S. Congress. Senate. Committee on Equal Opportunity. Hearings
    before the select committee on Equal Education Opportunity
    of the U.S. Senate, 91st Congress, 1st sess., 1970.

U.S. Department of Commerce, Bureau of the Census. <u>General Social and Economic Characteristics of the United States</u>, Publication P.C. (1)-C1. Washington, D.C.: U.S. Government Printing Office, 1972.

U.S. Department of Justice, Community Relations Service. <u>Annual Report</u>. Washington, D.C.: U.S. Government Printing Office, 1971.

U.S. Department of Justice, Immigration, and Naturalization Service. <u>Annual Report</u>. Washington, D.C.: U.S. Government Printing Office, 1972.

COURT CASES

Ashbacker v. The Federal Communications Commission, 326 (U.S.) 327, 330 (1945).

Banzhaf v. The Federal Communications Commission, 405 F. 2d 1082 C.A.D.C. (1968).

Chicago Joint Board, Amalgamated Clothing Workers v. Chicago Tribune Co., 307 F. Suppl. 422 (1970).

Citizens Committee v. The Federal Communications Commission, 18 RR 2d 2021 (1970).

Josef v. The Federal Communications Commission, 404 F. 2d 207 (1968).

New York Times Co. v. Sullivan, 376 U.S. 245 (1964).

Office of Communications, United Church of Christ v. The Federal Communications Commission, 359 F. 2d 997 (1966).

United States v. Midwest Video Corp. 441 F. 2d 1322 (8th Cir. 1971).

FRANCISCO JOSE LEWELS, Jr., attended the public schools in El Paso and then went to Texas Western College (now the University of Texas at El Paso), where he majored in journalism and was graduated in 1966. During his college years, he financed his education by working in public relations and advertising, first at deBruyn Advertising Agency and later at Bill/Lynde Public Relations. Upon graduation he entered the Army as a second lieutenant, attended the U.S. Army Aviation School, and then served a year in the Republic of Vietnam as a reconnaissance pilot during the Vietnam war. He holds the Bronze Star and the Air Medal with oak leaf cluster. In Vietnam, he also served as the public information officer for the 17th Combat Aviation Group.

He returned to the U.S. as a captain in October 1968 and worked as a writer/editor for the U.S. Army Aviation Digest Magazine at Fort Rucker, Alabama, for two years, while completing a master's degree in education at Troy State University. Upon completion of the degree, he accepted a scholarship from the University of Missouri and began working on a Ph.D. degree in mass communication. He served as the publications editor at the Freedom of Information Center for two years, while completing his course work, and then spent the summer of 1972 conducting the research for his dissertation as a summer intern with the U.S. Department of Justice in Washington, D.C. He is now chairman of the Department of Journalism at the University of Texas at El Paso.

RELATED TITLES
Published by
Praeger Special Studies

USES OF THE MASS MEDIA BY THE URBAN
POOR: Findings of Three Research Projects,
with an Annotated Bibliography.

> Bradley S. Greenberg and Brenda
> Dervin, with the assistance of Joseph
> R. Dominick and John Bowes

ADMINISTRATION OF THE FREEDOM OF
INFORMATION ACT: An Evaluation of
Government Information Programs under the
Act, 1967-72

> House Subcommitte on Foreign
> Operations and Government Infor-
> mation; Foreword by Representative
> William S. Moorhead

POLITICAL SOCIALIZATION OF CHICANO
CHILDREN: A Comparative Study with
Anglos in California Schools

> F. Chris Garcia

DEVELOPMENT ON A HUMAN SCALE:
Potentials for Ecologically Guided Growth
in Northern New Mexico

> Peter van Dresser

RACE MIXING IN THE PUBLIC SCHOOLS

> Charles V. Willie, with Jerome
> Beker